IN$ATIABLE

IN$ATIABLE

THE RISE
AND RISE OF THE
GREEDOCRACY

STUART SIM

REAKTION BOOKS

Published by Reaktion Books Ltd
Unit 32, Waterside
44–48 Wharf Road
London N1 7UX, UK
www.reaktionbooks.co.uk

First published 2017

Copyright © Stuart Sim 2017

Printed and bound in Great Britain by TJ International, Padstow, Cornwall

A catalogue record for this book is available from the British Library

ISBN 978 1 78023 734 3

CONTENTS

PREFACE

The exploits of the character Gordon Gekko in Oliver Stone's film *Wall Street* (1987) have become absorbed into our general culture, particularly his notion that greed is a socially desirable trait. He is adamant that 'greed is good', and that anyone trading on the stock market should operate by this principle without feeling in the least bit guilty about it – because he most definitely does not. For him, greed is the very driving force of life: it is what makes individuals tick. Gekko notwithstanding, not too many people would be prepared to agree with the principle that 'greed is good' – at least, not publicly. Greed has essentially negative connotations, bringing to mind misers and ruthless capitalists, and few would want to be described in that way. Their actions, however, might tell an entirely different story, and it is those actions that, as this book will illustrate, link the worlds of finance, business, economics, international sport and colonial and neocolonial empires. Underlying all such activity is something even closer to our own individual experience: human nature. To study greed is to look deeply, possibly more deeply than we might find entirely comfortable, into the darker recesses of human psychology, where our less desirable traits are to be found.

Greed can be disguised behind a wide range of human activities that individuals can claim are socially beneficial – although not always sincerely. When these activities are scrutinized more carefully, however, they can be revealed as much more problematic.

As a case in point, entrepreneurs, and the business community in general, argue that without their efforts we would all be much poorer. They state that the profits they gain personally as a result are a just reward for the valuable economic growth they promote, which benefits society by creating jobs and improving living standards for all. This is essentially the rationale put forward for neoliberal economics, and it does seem to justify greed no matter how it is described – a necessary evil perhaps, but necessary all the same. Avarice may be considered one of the Seven Deadly Sins, but critics would say that it is necessarily the driving force behind the current-day stock market, and so we are advised to put aside any objections we might have. To those involved in this area, the accusation of being greedy merely signifies jealousy at their talent for business and the success it has brought them (quite rightly, in their view). We should be content with the fact that all of us will gain, in some way or another, from a thriving economy. In a similar manner, the pharmaceutical giants can claim that the high prices they demand for new or improved drugs are justified, because it is in the public interest that they go on investing heavily in research to develop the next generation of these products: we all gain from this in terms of our quality of life.

While it cannot be denied that greed existed long before the rise of neoliberalism or the creation of the stock market, it can be argued that these generate a sociopolitical climate that appears actively to encourage greed. When considered objectively, it is hard not to reach the conclusion that speculation on the stock market is simply a form of gambling – a trait that is usually frowned upon in other walks of life. Lose money on the stock market and you might well elicit some sympathy from your circle of acquaintances; lose it in a casino, and you would be far less likely to. Like it or not, however, the stock market is one of the primary foundations of modern society, meaning that both greed and gambling are also deeply embedded. The case for and against greed is not as straightforward as it may initially appear.

Greed might therefore even be considered a socially beneficial drive – arguably with its roots in the survival instinct, which would make it a very basic human trait indeed. Any investigation into the subject of greed has to bear this latter aspect firmly in mind. Perhaps greed played a key role in the evolution of our species, guaranteeing that only the very fittest – and best provisioned – survived? Even misers could claim that being careful with money makes it easier to survive if hard times ever hit, as we know can only too easily happen to anyone. Greed would seem to be part of our psychological make-up and our cultural heritage – as in the case of colonial and neocolonial greed (see Chapter Seven) – and we need to come to terms with that. By taking a journey through greed's history, we shall discover just what such an accommodation demands of us.

INTRODUCTION:
WHY IS GREED AN ISSUE?

G reed is an issue that has gained prominence in the public realm in recent years, and that calls for some attention. But why is it an issue, and what role is it playing in our culture? Is it always good, as Gordon Gekko maintains in the film *Wall Street*, or only within certain parameters? This is a central question for our society, and the one that will be explored over the course of this book.

In the first place, greed's current prominence can largely be attributed to the excesses of the global financial sector, which has become reckless in its pursuit of ever-greater profits, pushing risk-taking to its limits – and then well beyond – in the early 2000s. Success in this endeavour has led to some quite obscene salaries and annual bonuses for bankers and traders, and these can only be explained by the promptings of greed, the 'inordinate, insatiable greed' that the American author Frank Norris regarded as such a depressing feature of modern life.[1] Annual bonuses of more than many people will make in their entire lifetime can hardly be explained in any other way, since they go well past any notion of need. The power they can grant to those whom the public pejoratively term 'fat cats', who have scant concern for the welfare of others outside their circle, can soon become addictive, and it is instrumental in creating a 'greedocracy'. It is this system that Tom Wolfe is mocking in his satirical novel *The Bonfire of the Vanities* when he describes his protagonist, Sherman McCoy, reflecting in self-congratulatory fashion on his status as a high-profile bond trader regularly raking in sudden large amounts of cash: 'On Wall Street he and a few others – how many? – three hundred, four hundred, five hundred? – had become precisely that . . . Masters of the Universe. There was no limit whatsoever!'[2]

Yet sometimes we do appear to reach such a limit, the point at which the system simply ceases to cope, as in the credit crash of 2007/8 when it did so quite spectacularly. This was the greatest shock to the stock market since the Wall Street crash of 1929, when the world economy was left in a parlous state, unleashing a storm of protest against bankers and financiers as the 'Great Depression' of the 1930s dragged on worldwide for years. The latest crisis has not, however, significantly altered the practices of the financial sector (the bonus system rolls inexorably on), and the inequality the sector serves to foster has become a topic for much anguished debate among both cultural commentators and politicians around the globe. The greedocracy may be thriving, but clearly the rest of us are not. Some influential economists now consider this growing inequality to be the greatest problem facing global society today, and are critical of the socioeconomic theory that underpins the current system: neoliberalism.

Paul Mason delivers a scathing critique of neoliberalism in his book about the credit crash, *Meltdown*, insisting that we have to treat it as an ideology rather than just an economic theory, 'a kind of secret religion for the super-rich' that is systematically impover-ishing the rest of us.[3] Since neoliberalism is based on a belief in unbridled competition – an apparently unshakeable belief among the converted, it would seem – social inequality is only too likely to be its outcome. It is a system in which if you win, you win big, creating an immediate wealth gap between you and the mass of the population that you can then manipulate in order to increase the gap even further – the assumption being that, for you anyway, there really is 'no limit'. Successful online entrepreneurs constitute high-profile examples of that process in action, often turning small start-ups into billion-dollar businesses within very short periods of time. Writing in 2009, Mason points out that 'the real wages of the average male U.S. worker are today below what they were in 1979 – and for the poorest twenty per cent, much lower.'[4] The book's subtitle proclaims 'the end of the age of greed', but from the vantage point of several years on that can only be described as over-optimistic, and it can feel like we are sliding back instead to the days of 'Buddy, Can You Spare a Dime?' Unemployment continues to be a massive social problem, and real wages are still falling throughout the major Western economies. For another eminent economist, Paul Krugman, it is not so much 'the end of the age of greed' we are witnessing as 'the return of depression economics', in an era worryingly 'reminiscent of the 1930s'.[5]

Neither is this just a twentieth-century problem. Charles Dickens presents us with a superbly realized example of the nineteenth century's 'age of greed' in the character of Ebeneezer Scrooge, whose name has since become a byword for the trait (as has Shakespeare's Shylock). Scrooge is someone who has gone beyond the socially acceptable parameters of greed: 'a squeezing, wrenching, grasping, scraping, clutching, covetous old sinner!', as his author introduces him.[6] Going further back in European history, greed was a vice that much concerned medieval and early modern European culture, with Christianity being very critical of such a worldly pursuit, which was seen as highly detrimental to one's spiritual prospects. (One wonders what the medieval Church would make of modern-day market traders of the Gordon Gekko variety.) Avaricious misers are depicted in many famous paintings of the period, such as Hieronymus Bosch's *Death and the Miser* of c. 1485–90.

The Church could, however, be hypocritical itself when it came to money, and was quite capable of displaying greed in the way that it compiled wealth during this period. Holy relics, for example, were a considerable source of income, being sold by the Church throughout Europe, much of the time under false premises, since their authenticity was very open to question. Pardons and indulgences were also freely on sale to those who could afford them. Even within the Church itself, there could be opposition to such practices, with some senior figures warning that it gave the impression that, as the cultural historian Michael Pye suggests, 'God did things in return for money, like forgive sin.'[7] Even worse was the fact that God appeared to implicitly favour the rich in these transactions; the more you spent, the more of your sins would be excused. A greedy God would be the antithesis to everything that Christianity claimed to stand for. Neither did the system encourage the idea that poverty was no barrier to salvation (as the poor were always being told by their priests). That would hardly seem to be the case considering that you could buy a pardon for your sins. The Church was playing a dangerous game with doctrinal principles. In our own time the Vatican Bank has been accused of shady financial dealings on several occasions, and large international institutions in general do appear to have generated greedy behaviour within their ranks on a fairly regular basis throughout history.

Episodes such as these eventually pass into history, and reform may or may not come about, but the critical point is that similar examples of institutional greed can be found in almost any era. A few years ago it could have been the scandal over UK MPs' expenses, which was met by a chorus of denials from those accused, some of whom were subsequently found guilty of misusing their allowances and expenses (to their shame, one hopes, but with the greedy one can never know). Public life will invariably yield up examples of greed among those placed in positions where financial temptation could occur, and it is almost certain that the future will have its share of such examples to add to the record. Why greed survives is as interesting a question to ponder as why the majority of us consider it to be so unethical. Why do so many succumb to it, and why does it seem to take root so easily in institutional contexts?

We know, too, that societies throughout history have been plagued by crime in all its various guises, and ours is no exception, providing evidence of just how ingrained greed is in our nature. So much criminal activity – certainly theft and robbery – is fuelled by greed and a desire for someone else's possessions. Cybercrime is but the latest example of greed's ingenuity, its ability to adapt itself to any environment and exploit whatever technological or cultural developments may arise. No system appears to be immune to crime, which always seems to find ways of siphoning off wealth that belongs to someone else. Nor does there ever seem to be any shortage of willing recruits to crime's ranks, regardless of the penalties that society puts in place for those who are caught. Looting regularly breaks out in the aftermath of riots or natural disasters, as if the criminal impulse merely requires the right kind of opportunity to present itself, such as empty or temporarily abandoned shops and houses, to prompt it into action. And we never seem to tire of reading about the exploits of criminals either, with crime fiction being one of the most popular literary genres in the world, and a perpetually attractive topic for both filmmakers and television producers. Criminal greed clearly fascinates us.

It could be argued that it is greed that propels the financial system and the bulk of entrepreneurial activity around the world, so in one sense it can be said to have a significant social value – when the system is working well, that is. What corporate entity or business tycoon does not want to increase their gains, and to go on doing so year after year, without fail? From that perspective it can perhaps reasonably be argued that 'greed is good', because collectively our standard of living is very much dependent on the success of the business sector. When recessions hit, it is not just businesses that suffer: nearly everyone else down the line does too, and the further down the line people are, the more vulnerable they are. When we express our hopes for an economic recovery, we could also be said to be hoping, quite unwittingly of course, for a resurgence of greed. The critical factor is how far the notion of 'greed is good' is taken, and whether all manifestations of financial greed are to be considered acceptable. Gordon Gekko, Sherman McCoy and their ilk may not choose to recognize that a limit exists, but it does and it soon becomes apparent to the rest of us when it has been reached.

Eventually, it is an issue concerning profit, the ultimate aim of financial greed: should it be subject to at least some sociopolitically monitored limitation to prevent stock market chaos? The question has to be put because when greed spirals out of control it can have devastating effects on the body politic. We are, after all, still mired in fiscal austerity several years after the credit crash, with no immediate end in sight for a weary public worn down by the effects of constant cutbacks in almost every area of their lives. Is it the case then that greed is acceptable, but only up to a certain point? And who sets that point and on the basis of what criteria? These have become critical questions for society, and no consensus as to how to resolve the situation has yet emerged. Given that neoliberals have enthusiastically embraced austerity (for others rather than for themselves, as the continuation of the bonus system so tellingly indicates), it may be some time yet before such a consensus does form and limits are implemented. There is all the more reason, therefore, to keep highlighting the problem and pushing it forward for debate.

Financial greed is not, however, the only form of greed that has a profound effect on our lives. We speak also of greed for food and greed for fame, as well as greed for resources in general: 'Masters of the Universe' can adopt many guises. An identifying factor in each instance is self-centredness, and this is usually subject to some degree of social control – but only if it starts to impact negatively on the lives, and rights, of others. Greed is a type of desire, and desire is not necessarily to be regarded as an antisocial drive. Ambition is fuelled by a desire for some kind of personal benefit, although it will be looked on with greater approval if it leads to wider social benefits. The exploits of business entrepreneurs will be judged on the basis of how they benefit society, and this can also be true of the arts. Individuals seek not only financial benefits, but emotional and spiritual ones and the work of creative artists carries such emotional and spiritual significance for a society as a whole. Ambition to achieve certain goals, or to outdo one's peers in the field, is often what motivates the creative artist, and it tends to be applauded: its ultimate social value can be recognized and appreciated. Entrepreneurs who develop socially useful products or services win similar plaudits. This could be seen as the acceptable face of greed, although public admiration for these entrepreneurs tends to fade somewhat when their fortunes start to soar into the billions and keep on growing. At that point, many members of the public begin to wonder how much money any one person ever really needs – or can realistically use. Looking at the fortunes, and careers, of the most successful, however, one has to assume that for some of our fellows no amount of money is ever going to be enough to satisfy them totally. They may not choose to label their desire insatiable greed, but from the outside it bears an uncanny resemblance.

In trying to persuade the public that he would be an appropriate choice for the u.s. presidency, Donald Trump has even used the argument that since he is already rich he can finance his own campaign and will not have to be dependent on backers, who would expect 'favours' for their financial backing:

> 'My whole life has been money,' he declared. 'I want money, I want money. Greed. I was greedy, I want more money, more money. Now they come up, "Donald, I'd like to give you $10m for your campaign." I go: "I don't want it."
>
> 'It's hard, because my whole life, I take money, take money. Now, I'm going to be greedy for the United States. I'm going to take and take and take.'[8]

In a country like America, where election campaigns traditionally require huge expenditure on activities like advertising (whether at national or local level), 'favours' are only too likely to enter into the process if candidates do not have a personal fortune to fall back on, and in this respect many may well think Trump has a valid point. He is not the only rich would-be politician who has used this line of argument, which puts another spin on the 'greed is good' notion: it apparently renders you the only kind of politician who can be trusted. Greed as a qualification for political office is not a particularly comforting thought, however, and it hardly seems to be in the spirit of democracy.

Ultimately, the issue turns on how far we are willing to allow self-centredness to go in the public realm, and what restrictions we think are socially acceptable to place on its expression. Laissez-faire economics enthusiastically encourage financial greed, whereas Marxist economics seek to eradicate it – with both claiming to be doing so for the common good. A very different conception of the self, and its social role, is involved in the respective theories. Societies are generally able to find some middle ground between the two extremes, and problems only occur when a society lurches to one extreme or the other for any sustained length of time. Communism was one such notable lurch; neoliberalism could be taken as its polar opposite. So the political aspect of greed must also be addressed. Nations can be greedy, as the history of nineteenth-century colonialism, and the mad scramble for resources that it involved on a global scale, demonstrates all too clearly. This is one form of greed that has had long-lasting and adverse effects, which are still at play in the twenty-first century. Many of the geopolitical tensions that currently plague our world derive from precisely that greed for resources (as in the Middle East), and solutions are proving thin on the ground. Neither have such attitudes disappeared altogether from Western culture. Neoliberalism is often accused of operating in a neocolonialist manner in its attitude towards the developing world, which is exploited for both its material and human resources for the benefit of the West – and, increasingly, for certain privileged Western groups in particular. Major corporations, investors and shareholders are by far the primary gainers from the globalization process. For all the high-minded reasons given for instituting it as a system for world trade, the effect of greed in all too many cases has been to turn globalization into colonialism by other means.

Greed is an issue for several reasons, therefore, and we really ought to be considering why that is so and what it says about us. What is the case for it, and what is the case against it? And how has the case been made either way throughout history? Such an enquiry will lead us not just into the realm of economics – the theories of Adam Smith versus those of Karl Marx, for example – but into politics, religion, psychology, social philosophy and the creative arts. As far as the latter goes, literature, art and more recently film all constitute particularly rich sources of representation of both the greedy and the plight of their victims. This book will investigate greed across its myriad manifestations and from a variety of positions and historical viewpoints, in order to analyse greed and to consider what, if anything, we can do about its stubborn persistence in our culture. The apparently insatiable appetite of the greedocracy for more and more wealth must be dealt with urgently.

1
TO DEFEND OR NOT
TO DEFEND GREED?

Although I have alluded briefly to some reasons why greed could be seen as a socially beneficial phenomenon, it is harder as a rule to make a sustained case for, than against, greed. Aside from the standard objections about being antisocial and exploitative of others, this is partly because it is so often disguised as something more benign by those who exhibit the trait, the motive being to deflect any criticism from the public by claiming to be proceeding from reasons other than the purely self-centred. It is not always immediately apparent, therefore, that we are actually dealing with greed. In my own part of the UK, a case concerning the development of greenbelt land for housing, a contentious topic throughout the country, provides an instructive example of how greed may be masked. The area's planning authorities, paying heed to protests from local residents, are resisting the proposal by a housing company to build a new estate on the land, pointing out the benefits to public health and well-being of maintaining a greenbelt area around large conurbations, as is common practice in most Western cities. These are persuasive arguments, one would think, but the housing company has cleverly played up to the public as well, insisting that their goal is to provide affordable housing for families in a pleasant area well away from the congestion, pollution and noise of the city. A project of this nature would also, of course, create jobs, no small consideration in an era of austerity and high unemployment, and this is signalled prominently in the planning application.

Profit is never mentioned by the company in question, although of course it is precisely that, rather than the public good (a nebulous concept at best in the private sector), which is the real impetus behind the application. That is why they feel a disguise of some sort is called for if the public is to be brought onto their side; hence their claim to be supplying something that the public should welcome. If profit were taken out of the equation they would be highly unlikely to show any interest in the project at all. Even if we all understand that this is the way the world works, however, we tend to shy away from acknowledging it too directly.

As populations increase in countries like the UK, fairly heavily populated as it already is, the greenbelt will no doubt continue to be a controversial issue, creating many animated confrontations in its wake. Cases are cropping up in the local and national media on a regular basis, as housing stock runs short with demand steadily rising. Fracking is another activity that is beginning to have the same effect, putting profit and the environment in open conflict with each other. This happened before on a large scale in the nineteenth century, with the spread of industrialization throughout the countryside leaving behind a badly scarred landscape that is still evident in many places today, even if, in the wake of globalization, deindustrialization has now set in for many once important manufacturing centres. The fracking lobby, however, with substantial backing from the UK government, does appear to be winning the battle so far, with the usual justifications being trotted out about creating jobs and helping the local economy. Various areas of the country have been earmarked for exploration, and work is underway in some places, despite much local opposition. There seems to be no going back now; it is just a question of how extensive the operation eventually becomes – as well as how damaging to the natural environment. The industry is already a going concern in countries such as the USA, where it is beginning to be regarded as a key element in the nation's future energy supply, significantly cutting its dependence on oil imports.

As long as we remain oil- and gas-greedy then this industry will continue to grow – as will the environmental consequences.

Energy suppliers are always on the lookout for new sources of profit, driven by the fact that there seems to be an insatiable appetite for their product to provide the lifestyle that people in most countries want. In this context there is no incentive to be environmentally minded. We are all implicated in this situation to at least some extent, since we all use energy and are showing little sign of willingness to reduce our usage significantly. The Western lifestyle is constructed around affordable and constantly accessible energy. That explains why drilling for oil in the Arctic, which poses yet more – potentially very serious – problems for the environment, is also going ahead despite a growing campaign of public protest. We protest, but continue to consume greater amounts of energy nevertheless. Environmental groups such as Greenpeace have issued dire warnings about the possible negative effects of oil exploration in the Arctic area, but the big oil companies have turned a deaf ear to such entreaties – or have claimed that environmentalists are exaggerating the likely risks. Profit does not give up easily.

Nevertheless, it is still possible to put forward an argument that the pursuit of profit can lead to public good when it provides employment and facilities for general use; although that cannot, and should not, always excuse any adverse effect this might have on the environment. It is undeniably the case that the standard of living has improved substantially over the last century or so, and it has to be assumed that a profit-oriented ideology has played its part in that process. Whether it is still doing so under an austerity-oriented economic regime is another matter entirely, but the point stands all the same. All of us are taking advantage of the greed shown by others (corporations or individuals), whether in terms of our jobs, what we buy as consumers or the energy we use. It therefore becomes a plausible defence for greed that we like the positive effect it has on our lifestyle, and that should give us pause for thought.

Despite this possible defence, most people are far likelier to be persuaded by arguments against greed – although that is not the same thing as saying that they would never exhibit such behaviour themselves. Who can honestly say they have never performed a greedy action, no matter how minor it may have been, even if it was only as a child? Children often have to be schooled out of the more obvious types of greed they display – grabbing the largest slice of cake, for example, or refusing to share with others. But we are all capable of reverting to behaviour like this on occasion, even if we know that it is antisocial to act in such a fashion. Have you ever deliberately taken the largest slice of cake as an adult? Or the last sandwich on the plate, or drink on the table, at a party? Have you fought to lay your hands on the last dress or shirt of its kind left on sale at a bargain price in a department store? Failed to share something you decided you would rather keep all for yourself instead? I suspect a lot of us have done some of these things at some time (maybe even most of them) and probably not agonized over it too much afterwards, or perhaps at all.

All of this does suggest that greed is a trait present in our make-up: 'a universal characteristic of individual human beings', as the philosopher Stewart Sutherland has insisted.[1] Arguably this could be the result of greed playing a part in human evolution; perhaps greed for resources helped ensure the survival of the fittest? Darwin's ideas are often employed by apologists for laissez-faire capitalism – where businesses compete against each to see who is the fittest to survive economically – to explain this aspect of our behaviour. Critics tend to regard this as a simplistic reading of Darwin, however, and it is worth remembering that Marx drew a very different conclusion from his work, regarding capitalism as just one stage in our social evolution that would eventually be surpassed by communism. Politically speaking, right and left are still divided on this issue today. The former regard greed as a socially beneficial trait, one that drives the economy on; whereas for the latter it is something to be overcome for the greater good.

There is no disagreement over greed being an element of human nature, however, only over how much latitude we should extend it. If greed is innate then the actions of stock market investors could be considered simply magnified examples of this 'universal characteristic'. It is entirely possible that almost any of us could act in the manner of a big-time speculator, focused solely on personal gain and prepared to take the necessary steps to win out over our competitors (and take satisfaction in the achievement), if we ever found ourselves placed in that situation with the means at our disposal to do so. Most of us will never be in that situation, but it is a worrying thought even so: an indication that greed is a spectrum upon which we are all situated at some point or other, and that it might be quite easy to move towards the higher end if the opportunity ever presented itself.

Most of us seem to have the gambling instinct, as the thriving betting industry attests, so it would probably not be difficult to awaken it in such circumstances. Now that gambling opportunities are so widespread on the Internet, for example (with all the negative implications this has for professional sport when players are persuaded to cooperate with gamblers for payment), many have been drawn into gambling who would probably not set foot in a betting shop or casino. Now that it is so easy to place a bet from home at the press of a key, it can seem to exert an almost irresistible appeal for some. It does just that for Pal Fagerland, the protagonist of the Norwegian writer Tore Renberg's novel *See You Tomorrow*, and Pal proceeds to make an awful mess of his life as a result, having run up debts he can never realistically repay on his modest salary as a local government officer. Being the head of a one-parent family does not help either. He confesses to some crooks, whom he has turned to for assistance in his plight, that he needs one million Norwegian krone (about £76,000) to clear his debts, but he is still running them up at the same time: 'Lose. Lose. Lose. Continue. Continue. Continue. Personal Loan, maxed-out card.'[2] Gambling is speculation in all but name, wherever it is practised – betting that next time around you will beat the system, stock market or otherwise. Greed always comes into the equation somewhere along the line when we are trying to gain something for nothing.

Identifying greed with capitalism is standard Marxist practice, and some of Marxism's most savage attacks on the concept come in the form of the musicals *The Threepenny Opera* (1928) and *The Rise and Fall of the City of Mahagonny* (1930), by Bertolt Brecht and Kurt Weill. The first is a reworking of John Gay's eighteenth-century play *The Beggar's Opera*, which is itself full of instances of greed. *The Threepenny Opera* pictures begging being turned into a business that preys on the public; the capitalist imperative, and the greed that motivates it, having infiltrated through to all levels of society without exception. Taken in hand by Jonathan Jeremiah Peachum, the entrepreneur running London's begging trade, and then clothed appropriately in rags and made up to look as if ravaged by poverty or illness, the 'destitute' and 'maimed' spread through the city, conning its citizens into extending charity to them. As the text describes the set-up: 'In order to combat the increasing hard-heartedness of men, Mr J. Peachum, man of business, has opened a shop where the poorest of the poor may acquire an appearance that will touch the stoniest of hearts.'[3] As is only to be expected, Peachum does very well out of the exploits of his band of beggars. It appears that as long as it yields a decent profit, any 'trade' can be acceptable. None of those involved in the begging business seems to be particularly bothered by any moral qualms about the career they have chosen; it is just one more way of playing the laissez-faire economic system, of being an entrepreneur, neither better nor worse than any other trade as long as one is prepared to examine it dispassionately enough.

In examining *The Threepenny Opera*'s source of inspiration in *The Beggar's Opera*, it is clear that Brecht has been very faithful to the tone of the original, which is just as cynical about the morals of its time, as Peachum's opening song reveals:

Through all the employments of life
Each neighbor abuses his brother;
Whore and rogue they call husband and wife;
All professions be-rogue one another.
The priest calls the lawyer a cheat;
The lawyer be-knaves the divine;
And the statesman, because he's so great,
Thinks his trade as honest as mine.[4]

Peachum goes on to claim that he sees no reason to feel ashamed of what he does for a living, since everyone else in his society is busily engaged in exploiting others for their own gain, just as he is. No one can be taken at face value, and hypocrisy is the hallmark of the times: 'A lawyer is an honest employment; so is mine. Like me too he acts in a double capacity, both against rogues and for 'em; for 'tis but fitting that we should protect and encourage cheats, since we live by them.'[5] In other words, greed infiltrates every aspect of society, and it spawns corruption as it goes; everyone cheats in their own way, as their circumstances allow. Both Gay and Brecht may be writing fiction, but the facts are not necessarily all that different in reality. We only have to consider the many public scandals of both the eighteenth century and our own, to recognize that neither author is letting his imagination run too far away with him in his cynicism. It is hard not to be cynical after the credit crash and the recent revelations of bribery and financial malpractice among high-ranking officials of the Fédération Internationale de Football Association (FIFA) and the International Association of Athletics Federations (IAAF), especially given the repeated denials of corruption by all the main figures involved.

Mahagonny takes an even harder line on capitalism. Here we are presented with Brecht's eccentric vision of America: a society constructed wholly on the notion of greed, a society in which money is the sole arbiter of all human behaviour. It is no accident that

Brecht chose America for the exercise, since it was a country fast building a reputation for being utterly obsessed with financial success, and known for its cut-throat business world in which fortunes could be made and lost at breakneck speed. This was the aftermath of the 'roaring twenties', when the stock market boom was generating a condition of mass greed in the nation that climaxed with the catastrophic Wall Street crash. The theme of capitalist greed is one that Brecht continually returned to in his work (as in his best-known play, *Mother Courage and Her Children*, written in 1939). Both the moral code and the legal system in Mahagonny are based on wealth: to have wealth is to be a valued member of society, not to have it is to be considered immoral. How the wealth has been obtained is immaterial to those with goods and services to sell, their main concern being to separate the wealthy from their cash as rapidly as they possibly can; supply meets demand, with no questions asked. Once the cash has gone, however, as the character of Jimmy Mahoney discovers all too swiftly, the individual is reduced to the status of a pariah, and can no longer depend on any help at all from his erstwhile friends and acquaintances, who will drift away one by one. The other's misfortune is to be shunned in a society that worships wealth. Mahagonny is in Brecht's view the quintessential capitalist 'paradise', where to be without money is a sin. (Even if we think this is stretching a point, having to claim welfare can often be regarded in a similar light nowadays, as if being poor and needing financial support is entirely the individual's fault rather than an effect of economic circumstances. Right-wing politicians are particularly prone to holding, and broadcasting, such views about those who are unemployed, as is the right-wing press. Poverty carries that kind of stigma in an austerity culture.)

When Jimmy and his friends arrive from Alaska, having laboured hard there for seven years to build up their savings, they are welcomed with open arms by the city's business community, who are ready and willing to meet their every need. There is nothing in the city that cannot be bought or sold, and conspicuous consumption is the norm, promoted aggressively at every turn. Friendship, sex and love are all treated purely as financial transactions, normal human relations having been excised from Mahagonny. Leocadia Begbick, effectively the city's procurer, makes this all very clear in offering the services of one Jenny to a member of the group: 'This is the girl for you, Mister O'Brien. If her hips ain't got no swing, your fifty bucks ain't worth shit on a shingle!'[6] O'Brien proceeds to haggle over the price, but Jimmy agrees to it and is rewarded with the pretence of love: all it requires is the $50 payment upfront. The friends proceed to have a riotous time, drinking, gambling and eating to excess, and with sex always available. It is a highly seductive lifestyle – for those who can afford it, and, crucially, while they can afford it. 'Love' will last just as long as the cash flow does.

This is of course the vision of a Marxist, always prone to believing the worst of the capitalist system and regarding it as leading inevitably to public and personal corruption. For those such as Brecht capitalism brings out the worst in human nature, providing a context in which greed openly flourishes at the expense of human relations. The capitalist characters in his plays are quite blatant about their motives. It is money they are after, and they will do whatever is necessary to get their hands on it. As Brecht wryly remarks of a shady businessman character in *The Threepenny Novel* (a follow-up to the musical): 'He never touched anything dirty; he always wore gloves.'[7] In real life, capitalist greed tends to be very adept at hiding itself behind apparently altruistic motives: the public good, a growing economy and the employment opportunities it offers, better-quality products or services to make our lives easier and more pleasurable. We all know the claims, and so did Brecht, but he refused to be taken in by them; for him they signified an antisocial desire to become wealthy at the expense of others. All of these justifications can be seen in the greenbelt development issue raised above, or in the case of fracking or Arctic oil exploration. The trouble is that most of the time we go along with this, or at least provide tacit consent by making use of what the commercial activity produces. Greed really does loom large in our lives whether we are all that conscious of it, or even on the lookout for it, or not; hence the need to be made aware of the effects it has had, and is continuing to have, on wider society.

At the risk of sounding overly moralistic, perhaps even puritanical, in our culture nowadays there is a lack of acceptance of deferred gratification. Removing this from our experience seems to be one of the main objectives of the commercial world, and it works on this task assiduously. Ordering online, for example, can cut delivery times dramatically, and companies boast about this in their advertising: one click and their products are on their way, often arriving within a matter of hours. With just one click it is also possible to place a bet via the Internet, and one need not wait long to find out the result of that either: success, or failure, is announced on screen in a very short space of time – as is the debit from your bank account if luck is not with you, as the odds suggest is the most likely outcome (as it is repeatedly for the hapless protagonist of *See You Tomorrow*). We have come to expect almost instant satisfaction of our desire to own things or do things, hence the general trend towards shops opening seven days a week, longer daily opening times and even 24-hour service in many cases. The Internet is certainly available 24 hours a day to aid in any activities you decide to undertake on the purchasing front. Delayed gratification is cast as an enemy to be banished from our experience, or at least from our shopping experience – and what could be more critical in a consumer society?

I am not saying that delayed gratification is a good thing in itself – that would be overly puritanical – but the more we are encouraged to think of it as an evil to have to wait for our desires to be gratified, the more likely it is that we could succumb to the greed for possession. The greedy do not want to wait. Patience plays no part in their make-up; they want their wishes to be fulfilled as speedily as possible – and to go on being so indefinitely. The commercial sector is only too happy to oblige. Greed flourishes in a culture that has come to view deferred gratification in such a negative light. Just notice how often advertisements for January sales urge us to hurry to take advantage of bargains while they are still in stock, doing their utmost to prove that there need be no delay in obtaining a desired item – not if you act on your impulse immediately. Each person's greed is in competition with that of all others chasing the same product, in the time-honoured tradition of sales. The necessary balance between acceptable and unacceptable greed is not being maintained in such instances, and it will have to be if we want to avoid self-centredness becoming the norm, both in our private behaviour and in the public realm. Neoliberals excepted, I suspect that quite a few of us would prefer it if there was rather less self-centredness around than there is currently is, instead of yet more – whether it is part of our evolutionary heritage or not. We should also note that greed, profit motive well to the fore, makes a very poor basis for human relations. Even if the situation in a capitalist society may not be quite as bad as Brecht claimed *all* of the time, it can be *some* of the time. The world of greed lays various traps for us, and it is important to understand how these function if we are to survive in this world with any integrity left to our name. Greed can cause misery and distress. The question before us is, how can we rein it in?

2

WHATEVER YOU DESIRE?
THE PSYCHOLOGY OF GREED

The seventeenth-century philosopher Thomas Hobbes thought that human beings were motivated by one overwhelming desire: the desire to survive. We are naturally egocentric individuals, according to Hobbes, concerned above all to guarantee our own personal security, which we would automatically do at the expense of others unless that drive is severely curbed by a strong political power able to make us submit, and ensure that we continue to submit, to its rule. Greed, however, could be seen as a manifestation of that selfishness even under the strongest of governments. Greed for resources leads to greater power over our fellow human beings the more we succeed in acquiring for ourselves, as every business tycoon is acutely aware. This is what the political philosopher C. B. Macpherson dubbed 'possessive individualism', and the right to it has been enshrined in our modern political system, where personal property is treated as all but sacrosanct. As Macpherson puts it: 'Political society becomes a calculated device for the protection of this property and for the maintenance of an orderly relation of exchange.'[1] This is a psychology of greed we can understand, even if we do not necessarily agree with it – as Marxists plainly do not, regarding it as the source of all our social problems. Personal ownership of property may be anathema to Marxists, but owning one's own home has become something of an obsession in Western society – and all the better if it includes a substantial garden, land of one's own. There are few who do not aspire to that condition.

Property ownership is a fundamental element of democratic society, which governments in the West are particularly keen to preserve, especially since it plays such a critical role in the economy. Mortgages are big business, and the banks are highly dependent on the turnover in this market to push up their profits and keep their shareholders happy, given that over time the profit margins on mortgages can be very considerable indeed, thanks to the interest charges levied. The downside is that when things get out of hand in the mortgage industry then the economy inevitably suffers from knock-on effects, as happened so dramatically in the 2007–8 credit crash with so-called 'sub-prime loans'. This turned into a classic example of 'inordinate, insatiable greed', and how it can all go quite horribly wrong. The banks flouted economic common sense with these loans, extended to low-income, high-risk parties, and we have all had to pay the penalty in years of austerity after the loanees proceeded to default en masse. The episode left the banking system in some considerable disarray. In many cases banks required bailouts from national government in order to remain in business, the rationale being that they were too big to fail and it would put the nation's entire economy severely at risk if that were allowed to happen. Given that the financial industry has always opposed government intervention in its affairs on the grounds that it distorts the workings of the free market, there is more than a hint of irony in this outcome. The system that it apparently despised had to come to its rescue. Not that this has dispelled greed from the industry, where it remains as much of a factor as ever; the desire to express this trait of greed is too deeply embedded in its participants to be thrown off course by any such temporary 'difficulty'. Hobbes would have recognized the state of mind involved only too well, as our basic nature showing through.

Desire in general has been a topic of much interest to modern philosophers, many of whom, like Gilles Deleuze and Félix Guattari, have come to treat it as a drive that ought to be given the widest possible scope for expression. Repression is taken to be an antisocial activity, in desire no less than in politics, and various arguments have been put forward for greater tolerance to be shown by society at large towards sexual desire. Michel Foucault took up that cause in terms of homosexuality, outlining how attitudes towards the practice had changed over the history of Western society from the classical period onwards, sometimes being more or less repressive depending on the cultural ethos of the times.[2] Much the same can also be said of official attitudes towards female heterosexual desire, which has traditionally been the subject of repression in patriarchal societies. While making it easier to express desire in sexual matters has generally been welcomed by wider society, it is more problematical to argue for complete freedom of expression for all desires – such as greed. When libertarianism is taken that far then it can have adverse effects on the general public, often weakening the social bond.

Deleuze and Guattari claimed that we should regard ourselves as 'desiring machines', and do our utmost to resist culture's attempt to tame and control us, thus preventing the satisfaction of our desires.[3] This follows on from the Freudian notion of 'the return of the repressed', which points out that desire can be suppressed but never wholly eradicated; it will find a way to break through eventually, and as Freud warns, not always in a positive way.[4] The repression is the product of 'an incompatibility ... between the ego and some idea presented to it', which the ego attempts to reject, but unsuccessfully: 'That idea is not annihilated by a repudiation of this kind, but merely repressed into the unconscious.'[5] Yet desire cannot be assumed always to be worthy of expression: sadists and psychopaths have a strong desire to hurt, or even kill, others and that is not in society's interest at all. Fascists have desires as we all do, but a society that enables the expression of these is the antithesis to what we conceive of as a modern liberal democracy. No matter how liberal a democracy may be, it still has to draw the line somewhere on what it will allow individuals to do.

There is also the question of which desires are the product of nature and which of nurture (greed being a pertinent example as the one most concerning us here), as well as the extent of latitude that society should grant either way. These are big questions that every society has to confront, regardless of what laws previous generations may have passed to regulate behaviour. Conduct that may have been considered acceptable in one historical period may be found overly restrictive, or alternatively overly tolerant, in another. The laws concerning homosexual activity provide an interesting case study in this respect. It was classified as a criminal act in the UK until 1967, but since then it has gained at least a modicum of public acceptance, up to the point of gay marriage being legalized in England, Wales and Scotland in 2014. This has been a clear victory for difference and diversity against the forces of discrimination. Changing attitudes towards drug use provide another interesting example. Take, for instance, the Victorian fondness for laudanum, which was openly on sale in British pharmacies until the mid-nineteenth century. Authors such as Thomas De Quincey and Wilkie Collins had no trouble procuring a regular supply for their habit, the former writing about it memorably in his *Confessions of an English Opium Eater*.[6] In fact, a surprising number of well-known public figures resorted to using laudanum on occasion, behaviour that would most likely provoke rebuke nowadays as setting a bad example. It is an issue that is never quite resolved, and which must be the subject of constant debate, with compromises having to be reached along the way, generation by generation. Our situation is no different in the twenty-first century.

Hobbes is somewhat infamous for his theory of the state and what would constitute the most efficient form of government, given his view of human nature. For Hobbes, the survival instinct was our primary drive, and it had the potential to be very socially disruptive, setting individuals against each other in perpetual competition, with self-interest their one and only concern. The individual was constantly striving to maximize his or her personal security, and would go to the utmost lengths possible to do so. In Hobbes's conception life was a bitter struggle to prevail, and human beings were, in their natural state, intensely self-centred and egotistical, focused on their own welfare to the exclusion of anything else. With all of us competing against each other in so strident a fashion, personal security is all but impossible to guarantee; the struggle never relents. This, Hobbes believed, was the problem faced by any civil society: how to maintain public order so that all of us would benefit in terms of our individual safety, rather than being under constant threat from the never-ending machinations of others.

Put this way, there is nothing particularly contentious about Hobbes's assumptions. Ensuring public order is one of the most basic concerns of every kind of state, in that without it the state can barely function at all. The form that order might take can vary, but it is always a primary consideration. Few of us would disagree with the necessity of this – a few anarchists excepted, perhaps. It is when we consider Hobbes's solution that problems start to emerge. Hobbes was doggedly opposed to any form of division of power. He considered democracy to be the worst possible form of government, being far too subject to the unpredictable vagaries of public opinion and competing factions. For Hobbes, difference and diversity were divisive factors that were to be kept out of politics at all costs, since they had the potential to lead to civil discord. He championed instead the notion of an absolute ruler with unlimited power over the nation's citizens: a system of government that we would describe now as dictatorial or totalitarian. Everyone in a Hobbesian state was deemed to have ceded all their natural rights in perpetuity to the reigning sovereign, and then his or her heirs in their turn. The sovereign's will could not be questioned: as the repository of all our individual rights, that privileged figure was granted the power to act with utter impunity. The alternative, as Hobbes saw it, was a condition of outright anarchy, with every individual striving to dominate their fellows – the dreaded 'state of nature', where 'every man is Enemy to every man' and no one could ever feel completely safe.[7] Harsh though absolute sovereignty could undoubtedly be, it was in Hobbes's view infinitely preferable to existence with no effective safeguards in place whatsoever, with danger lurking around every corner. Surrendering our natural rights was considered to be a price worth paying under the circumstances.

Hobbes's argument assumes that at base all human beings are motivated by a greed for power: power over others to make their own existence safer. Theoretically at least, that greed can never be wholly satisfied, everyone else being similarly motivated, and it is not exactly conducive to the smooth running of a society. Nation states often act in a power-hungry way, however, as the phenomenon of empire-building would suggest. There is no overall global sovereign power to keep all nations in line – the United Nations has very limited effectiveness in that regard, as it can exhort but not compel. As a result, disputes can, and regularly do, occur. War is, after all, a recurrent theme of human history, and there are several examples that could be cited at the time of writing, with greed for territory so often a major factor.

It does not take too much of a leap of the imagination to see the business world in a similar light. Tycoons certainly give the impression of being driven by the same kind of impulses, always scheming to expand their empires and exercise domination over all their competitors – a struggle that never really ceases. Modern history is full of such individuals, and the commercial world is designed to encourage this kind of behaviour. Nothing ever seems to be enough for the tycoon figure, who has to assume that his or her rival is continually plotting to cut their share of the market and overtake them in the power stakes. Constant vigilance is required if success is to be maintained; that is what a competitive environment demands of its participants. Relax that vigilance even for a while and you will quickly fall behind, because in this realm danger is thought to lurk around every corner. From the tycoons' perspective, therefore, greed becomes a necessary trait to develop, a survival mechanism in their equivalent of the 'state of nature'. Generally speaking, the public accepts that this is the way the business world has to operate if the economy is to grow and living standards are to improve. Perhaps greed really is necessary for the kind of society we have created, but this is not a particularly comforting thought.

Deleuze and Guattari created a considerable stir in the intellectual world with their two books on the subject of 'capitalism and schizophrenia', *Anti-Oedipus* and *A Thousand Plateaus* (published in the original French in 1972 and 1980 respectively), both of which claimed that the modern world was committed to the suppression of human desire, basically on ideological lines. The two volumes represented a sustained plea for resistance to be mounted to all the various institutional mechanisms designed to block desire in our culture, and took the novel, if on the face of it impractical, stance of recommending the cultivation of schizophrenic behaviour on the part of the individual as a way of attempting to outwit repression. They advocated schizophrenia with a particular twist, however, in that it was to have a political agenda. Deleuze and Guattari contrasted their version of schizophrenia with what they referred to as 'the artificial schizophrenic found in mental institutions: a limp rag forced into autistic behavior'; their schizophrenic was to be a much more subversive figure.[8] The goal was to frustrate institutional power, which sought to enforce conformity on the population in order to exercise control over it, programming people to act in predictable ways – as Hobbes thought was eminently desirable. Psychoanalysis was one of the means employed to this end, being based on the premise that there was a 'normal' personality, and that all variations from this were to be considered unacceptable. As Paul Verhaeghe has pointed out, this was to take 'normality as an ideal', meaning that 'ideological prescriptions of how mankind ought to be' were coming into play.[9] Diversity and difference were to be treated as enemies within, warning signs of ideological unreliability and thus a threat to social order.

Sigmund Freud's concept of the Oedipus complex made just such an assumption of a normal personality type, and became for Deleuze and Guattari a symbol of a wider trend at work within modern culture, which sought to eradicate nonconformist behaviour altogether. Nonconformity was perceived to be a threat by the ruling classes, whose collective power was dubbed 'Oedipus' by Deleuze and Guattari, who argued that 'Oedipus presupposes a fantastic repression of desiring-machines'.[10] They set themselves up to be the proponents of 'Anti-Oedipus' instead, recommending that we should reject the norms of behaviour put forward for us by the powers-that-be and act in an unpredictable manner that would baffle the system. As one of the translators of *Anti-Oedipus* succinctly remarks: 'What it attempts to cure us of is the cure itself.'[11] Only in this way would we be in a position to realize our desires fully, as our true nature wanted, to resist the greed for power over others that lay behind capitalism as a system, with Oedipus cast as one of its major agents of repression. Deleuze and Guattari took issue with the Freudian notion of desire as 'lack', and this idea of absence appears to be the way that greed generally presents itself: as a desire for something that is not currently in our possession, such as money, fame or power. For Deleuze and Guattari, desire is something much more positive than that, something that can, if it manages to escape repression, threaten the social and political order, and which is, in their opinion, to be welcomed.

Desire in our culture is, however, up against the 'body without organs', an entity comprising the antisocial traits of being 'the unproductive, the sterile, the unengendered, the unconsumable', and of 'appropriating for itself all surplus production' (as the individual in Hobbes's state of nature also seeks to do).[12] I have suggested elsewhere that modern-day capitalism would fit this description (Marx, too, had railed against the appropriation of surplus production); but it could in many ways describe greed, taken as an abstract entity, too.[13] It is clearly the case that greed seeks to appropriate all surplus production and eventually to become parasitic on the society it is operating within, steadily draining away society's resources for its own benefit. The greedy are constantly taking rather than giving, so are unproductive and sterile in that sense (an apt description of crime as well). It is an attitude well exemplified by the phenomenon of tax avoidance, especially among the wealthier classes, many of whom certainly do want to take more from and give less back to society if they can get away with it. Rather than allowing ourselves to become the slaves of such a project, Deleuze and Guattari recommend that we should embrace 'nomadism' instead, refusing to be tied down to any particular activity, way of life or set of ideas, in the manner of traditional nomadic tribes, wandering from place to place without any settled home.[14] Greed would find it much tougher to flourish in such a situation (financial greed anyway), and it would clearly unsettle the current world economic order, and the notion of a market-driven society, if nomadism were to become widespread. Whether such a lifestyle would suit our psychology nowadays is another question, even if it did hold out the promise of a greater freedom from social constraints.

Most of us would recognize, however, a need to rein in desire to at least some extent; otherwise social existence would very probably become totally chaotic. Nomadism sounds all very well and good, but I suspect few of us could countenance such a rootless lifestyle indefinitely – even if Deleuze and Guattari do intend it to be taken in a mainly metaphorical sense, a method of avoiding ideological dogmatism. Nor would developing a schizophrenic personality to elude the demands of our ideological system have great popular appeal. Unpredictability would soon become disorienting if carried to extremes, and it cannot be denied that human desire is capable of reaching some very unpleasant extremes, as evidenced by serial killing, ethnic cleansing or forced labour, for example. Challenging the system is one thing; putting the safety of your fellow human beings in jeopardy is surely something else altogether, and giving desire its head would almost undoubtedly have that effect – and probably quite rapidly too. As with greed, some compromises have to be reached over the issue of desire: when it is reasonable for desire to be expressed, as well as how, where and when it is not. Every society has to legislate for this to ensure at least a measure of public order; it may not have to go to the lengths suggested by Hobbes to achieve this, but it does have to put some constraints in place.

Freud's theories were designed to enable practitioners to treat conditions such as schizophrenia, and antisocial desires in general, not to encourage their untrammelled expression: in effect, to restore personal order in individuals by exploring through analysis the hidden causes for their behaviour within their subconscious drives. Deleuze and Guattari are right that behind this approach lies a conception of 'normal' personality and what constitutes a standard range of social behaviours – 'an ideal image of mankind'.[15] But not everyone will be convinced that this is such an undesirable a condition to be aspired to, nor quite so ideologically loaded. In fact, the notion of restoring a sense of normality in the individual is what lies behind many practically oriented contemporary therapies, such as cognitive behavioural therapy (CBT). Used by several health services, including Britain's NHS, CBT does not attempt the depth analysis favoured by Freudians, being more concerned with the practicalities of coping with everyday setbacks. It describes itself as a 'talking therapy' that aims to help the patient break down apparently overwhelming problems into smaller, more manageable parts. By Freudian standards, CBT is more like a quick-fix method, but it would be no more likely to meet with Deleuze and Guattari's approval than the older theory. Since both Freudianism and CBT are concerned with channelling human behaviour into predictable patterns, within accepted rules and social conventions, Deleuze and Guattari would see them both as being in the service of the dreaded 'Oedipus'.

Desire is obviously central to Freud's work, and he does equate it with a 'lack' of some object in the individual's life, something that the individual wishes to possess or control but is unable to (a line of thought that continues in the work of post-Freudian theorists such as the influential Jacques Lacan). Although, as Robert Bocock has pointed out, 'There is still a problem about how social scientists, including psychoanalysts and sociologists, can know what these bodily wishes and desires are,' never mind the individual reacting to the promptings of his or her unconscious.[16] The failure to achieve what one lacks can, Freud argues, lead to hysteria, particularly, he believed, among women (much to the displeasure, as you would expect, of several generations of feminist theorists). Positing that 'sexuality seems to play a principal part in the pathogenesis of hysteria as a source of psychical traumas and as a motive for "defence" – that is, for repressing ideas from consciousness,' Freud (and Josef Breuer, one of his associates in his early work) tended to see hysteria as a displacement of frustrated sexual desire, a somewhat desperate response occurring in the absence of its satisfaction.[17] They believed it was the 'lack' of this fulfilment, of an appropriate balance being in place between desire and fulfilment, that triggered not just hysteria but many other supposedly 'abnormal' psychological conditions. They argued that women, particularly young women, were more likely than men to have difficulty dealing with their sexual feelings:

> The tendency towards fending off what is sexual is further intensified by the fact that in young unmarried women sensual excitation has an admixture of anxiety, of fear of what is coming, what is unknown and half-suspected, whereas in normal and healthy young men it is an unmixed aggressive instinct.[18]

They believed there to be a greater incompatibility between ego and idea in this group, and thus a greater disposition towards repression that could subsequently lead to hysteria.

Freud held desire to be a much more problematical condition in women than it was in men, the sense of 'lack' much sharper; indeed, he went so far as to refer to female sexuality as a 'dark continent'.[19] Whether women are the delicate creatures that this implies, or inherently mysterious and unknowable, is a contention that feminists have disputed ever since, and it does betray a stereotypical view of gender: men as aggressive, women as passive. Nevertheless, a certain amount of support for Freudian theory overall can still be found in feminist circles. Juliet Mitchell, for example, puts forward the view that Freud was not so much defending patriarchal society as analysing it, meaning that feminists can still draw on his theories in their own researches into patriarchy.[20] From this perspective, the lack can to some extent be overcome, being largely a product of social conditioning. The hysteria is therefore a response to a situation that need not occur; it is not biologically determined.

The notion of lack (*manque*) plays an important role in Lacan's theory of desire, signalling for him, as one of his commentators has succinctly phrased it, 'a hole in being'.[21] In Lacan's formulation, 'man's desire is the desire of the other', and it consistently comes up against the experience of lack:

> A lack is encountered by the subject in the Other, in the very intimation that the Other makes to him by his discourse ... The desire of the Other is apprehended by the subject in that which does not work, in the lacks of the discourse of the Other.[22]

Even allowing for Lacan's notoriously dense writing style ('so polyvalent and ambiguous' as one his translators somewhat ruefully describes it),[23] the nature of that lack seems a particularly complex issue when it comes to women:

> 'Woman' is a signifier, the crucial property of which is that it is the only one that cannot signify anything, and this is simply because it grounds woman's status in the fact that she is not-whole. That means we can't talk about Woman. A woman can but be excluded by the nature of things, which is the nature of words.[24]

The argument becomes even more tortuous after that (for anyone who cares to brave it), but there is a definite sense of a 'hole in being' as an inescapable fact of existence, and as with Freud, in women's case lack is held to be a particularly complicated condition.

Leaving that gender issue aside, a 'hole in being' is the way that greed seems to affect those most smitten with it: as something missing in their identity that constantly nags away at them to be addressed, and that may never be completely satisfied. No matter how much they may succeed in accumulating, the sense of lack will not go away. As Lacan puts it, desire is 'what is invoked by any demand beyond the need that is articulated in it, and it is certainly that of which the subject remains all the more deprived to the extent that the need articulated in the demand is satisfied'.[25] Given that desire is such a critical part of our make-up (the part that turns each of us into a fully fledged subject in Lacan's view), situations where such deprivation is felt will continue to occur throughout every individual's life, and this can create the right conditions for greed to manifest and tempt us. 'The demand that goes beyond need' sums up greed very neatly.

3

IN THE RED CORNER, KARL MARX;
IN THE BLUE, ADAM SMITH:
THE ECONOMICS OF GREED

odern economic theory – originating with Adam Smith in the eighteenth century – does not condone greed as such, but it can encourage it in implicit ways nevertheless. The free market is constructed around the notion of the entrepreneurial self, and the corporate structures that arise from that, which encourage competition against others in order to gain, and maximize, profits. If only implicitly, therefore, an element of greed lies under the surface (if not very far under when it comes to stock market traders), and modern culture very much promotes a strong sense of selfhood to reinforce the impulse: C. B. Macpherson's 'possessive individualism' in robust action. Laissez-faire economics insists that this system will find its equilibrium if it is allowed to operate without any restrictive regulation being introduced by outside bodies – such as government, viewed as a very unwelcome presence in this area. The figure generally regarded as the key to the development of laissez-faire economics is Adam Smith, although what is often passed over by his modern-day followers is the fact that Smith himself, whose primary professional concern was ethics, also preached a need for social responsibility, which does not always sit well with the ways in which his economic theories have been adapted and applied since. If the market deteriorates into a free-for-all, then it soon becomes every individual for him- or herself and hang the consequences – not at all what Smith envisaged.

The major critic of laissez-faire economics is the philosopher Karl Marx, who was appalled at the effect it had on nineteenth-century society, where it generated gross inequality among the various classes and precious little in the way of social responsibility in recompense. Living conditions for the vast majority of the working classes were quite dreadful, with disease rife in the crowded urban centres, and until well into the century little in the way of environmental planning or health and safety regulation in the factories where they laboured. Whether Marx would have been happy at the way his theories have been adapted and applied since is also very open to question, but his opposition to the laissez-faire system was to become deeply engrained in communist doctrine. Officially at least, communism hated the market system and rejected it as a mode of running an economy (unofficially, a black market developed in most communist countries).

This is roughly how the debate has proceeded from Victorian times onwards. In the red corner, we have Karl Marx and his communist and socialist followers; in the blue corner, Adam Smith and his disciples through to the emergence of neoliberalism, the most widely adopted economic theory of our time (defended, appropriately enough, by such bodies as the Adam Smith Institute, a think-tank founded to propagate the cause of the free market). Once again, there are very different conceptions of the self involved, and the virtues and vices of each need to be carefully considered. At one end of the spectrum we have the sublimation of the self in the collective; at the other, rampant self-interest, with the collective left to fend for itself as best it can. In between, there are various combinations of the two: for example, social democracy, the 'third way' as adopted by the UK Labour Government from 1997 to 2010, Chinese 'state capitalism' and so on – as well many differing conceptions of what either position requires of us in terms of lifestyle. After the fall of the Soviet Union in 1991, self-interest may well be the dominant position nowadays, but the debate itself is very far from over. The hegemony exercised by self-interest is coming in for increasingly critical scrutiny in the twenty-first century, with its current obsession with austerity economics in the public sphere.

Adam Smith's objective in *The Wealth of Nations* (1776) was to address what he took to be the impediments to economic progress in his day, such as the monopoly system that was so widespread in British life at the time (in fact, throughout much of Western European society, including the colonies they were even then busily establishing around the globe). The existence of monopolies for certain goods or services, officially sanctioned by the ruling authorities, suppressed competition in trading the products involved. To thinkers like Smith, this made British economic life lazy, inefficient and non-innovative: 'Monopoly ... is a great enemy to good management, which can never be universally established but in consequence of that free and universal competition which forces everybody to have recourse to it for the sake of self-defence.'[1] There could be no stimulus to improve services or the quality of goods if there was a monopoly in place to supply these; and the public had no option but to accept whatever was on offer from the monopoly holders:

> A monopoly granted either to an individual or to a trading company has the same effect as a secret in trade or manufactures. The monopolists, by keeping the market constantly under-stocked, by never supplying the effectual demand, sell their commodities much above the natural price, and raise their emoluments, whether they consist in wages or profit, greatly above their natural rate. The price of monopoly is upon every occasion the highest which can be got.[2]

Smith felt that vigorous competition was the only way to break this cycle, and that the public good would best be served by individuals being allowed to follow their own self-interest without hindrance. Collectively such actions were to the benefit of society as a whole through the agency of the market; the individual producer 'intends only his own gain, and he is in this, as in many other cases, led by an invisible hand to promote an end which was no part of his intention'.[3] Self-interest could be defined in such instances, therefore, as 'good greed'. Good not just for the individuals involved in purchasing or selling these goods, but for all: the healthier the market, the higher the average standard of living was likely to be. Smith's treatise is one of the defining statements of individualism in modern life: the belief that if individual initiative is set free and given the opportunity to put its ideas into practice, then it will be better all round for everybody – efficiency and innovation will surely follow in its train. Liberal democracy is firmly committed to this belief.

The 'invisible hand' has been interpreted by the more enthusiastic followers of Smith to mean that there should be no restrictions placed on the workings of the market; the notion being that even if greed is in evidence in the latter, it will eventually prove to be to the benefit of society as a whole. From this perspective, much favoured by neoliberal economic theorists in recent years, there ought to be no checks placed on market trading, because these would only throw the 'invisible hand' off course. Markets must be allowed to find their own equilibrium, even if it can occasionally be a rocky ride on the way there. We should put our faith in the market's ability to respond to any crisis that may result, and these must always be assumed to be of a temporary nature; it will all come good eventually. We just have to be patient and let the 'invisible hand' do its work – which left to its own devices it assuredly will.

So goes the neoliberal economic narrative, yet we all know how greed can spiral out of control such that equilibrium can take a long time to be established. Modern economic history is full of depressions, recessions and market 'bubbles' that economies can take years to recover from, causing considerable hardship to much of the world's population along the way; as in the case of the 'Great Depression' of the 1930s, which was only overcome after sustained, and substantial, government help in both America and Europe.

Greed is the driving force behind such phenomena, and social conscience does not feature prominently in the decisions that, taken by enough players, can lead to a market implosion. The 'invisible hand' is just as capable of having a negative effect as a positive one. Neoliberal theorists will generally shrug off such an event as merely an aberration, the work of only a few rogue individuals, and will insist that the system itself is fundamentally very sound. Greed, however, never goes away and always manages to reassert itself, disturbing the system's balancing act. Unfortunately for the majority of us, it would seem that rogue individuals can always be found, primed to be on the lookout for an opportunity to make a 'killing' at the expense of their peers, and not too concerned about the legality of how they achieve that. The distinguished economist Joseph E. Stiglitz has also pointed out that 'even if Smith's invisible hand theory were relevant for advanced industrialized countries, the required conditions are not satisfied in developing countries', which lack the institutional infrastructure that a market needs in order to operate properly.[4] In that setting, greed has even more freedom to operate, and invariably makes use of it.

Although the market system has become more competition-based since Smith's day, it is interesting to note how easily it can still gravitate towards a condition of monopoly. Stiglitz feels this reveals a critical underlying flaw in laissez-faire theory: 'If competition were automatically perfect, there would be no role for antitrust authorities.'[5] Major multinationals have a tendency to absorb their smaller competitors and eventually come to dominate their field. Once they do, they are in a position to control those who supply them, and that can have the effect of driving smaller companies out of business – hardly what Smith's form of laissez-faire economics had in mind, since it undermines the 'free and universal competition' that he championed. This is an effect much in evidence nowadays, especially with the impact of globalization, which very much favours the larger organizations, with their highly developed infrastructures and considerable financial muscle. In the late nineteenth century there was a similar trend, particularly in the U.S., which ultimately prompted government intervention and the passing of antitrust laws to curb the power of the monopolies. But it is a recurring phenomenon under the free market system, for all its apparent commitment to the competition ethic: succeed in removing competition, and your own profits will proceed to soar. It has become even more of a problem nowadays with multinationals, who by locating themselves in tax havens outside their main countries of operation are often able to limit the amount of government intervention they might be exposed to.

There is another side to Smith, however, which identifies what could be called 'bad greed'. Smith was a professor of moral philosophy, and argued strongly in favour of a compassionate attitude towards one's fellow human beings, arguing that 'how selfish soever man may be supposed, there are evidently some principles in his nature, which interest him in the fortune of others, and render their happiness necessary to him.'[6] Stock market traders take heed, one feels moved to observe. Smith's ethical beliefs, 'a combination of Stoic and Christian virtues', as the editors of *The Theory of Moral Sentiments* describe them, emphasized how connected we are to others, not how self-contained.[7] Greed is not a compassionate trait, given that it involves putting self-interest before all other considerations and leaving others to deal with the after-effects; it is almost the definition of selfishness. Smith's ethics were founded on a very different principle, as we can note from sentiments such as the following: 'to feel much for others and little for ourselves . . . to restrain our selfish, and to indulge our benevolent affections, constitutes the perfection of human nature.'[8] Citing the 'invisible hand' as justification could be regarded as an evasion of the often negative consequences of allowing self-interest free rein. Egocentricity and compassion would seem to exclude each other. For Smith, on the other hand: 'We should view ourselves, not in the light in which our own selfish passions are apt to place us, but in the light in which any other citizen of the world would view us.'[9]

This is a lesson, however, that seems to evade most neoliberals, who are only too liable to put selfish passions at the centre of human conduct, as if they hold the answer to all our social problems.

Compared to Smith, neoliberalism offers us a very narrow vision of what a society should be, and it can be very selective in its interpretation of his economic theories. Even in *The Wealth of Nations* Smith allows that there are various 'unproductive' occupations that deserve to be subsidized by the state. As well as the sovereign and the armed forces, these include 'churchmen, lawyers, physicians, men of letters of all kinds; players, buffoons, musicians, opera-singers, opera-dancers, etc.'[10] Their labour is deemed to be unproductive in the sense that it 'produces nothing which could afterwards purchase or procure an equal quantity of labour' back, since 'the work of all of them perishes in the very instant of its production'.[11] How many of these 'unproductive labourers' there should be is a matter for conjecture; but Smith does appear to be removing legal, medical and cultural activity from the open market because of their intrinsic value to society as a whole. Neoliberalism, on the other hand, is opposed to such a policy, insisting that unproductive labour, other than operating the armed forces and the basic functions of government, should be subject to the rigours of the market; for the state to assume responsibility for this smacks of socialism. It is because of such views that Obamacare was opposed, and the NHS is under such pressure to privatize more and more of its services.

Karl Marx regarded greed as absolutely integral to capitalism, and his work from *The Communist Manifesto* (1848) through *Capital* (1867) was designed to show how this trait could be abolished for the public good. Communism was to be the socioeconomic system that would achieve this goal, with the means of production being brought under public control such that everyone gained from their output, rather than just an elite band of owners and shareholders. Between them, owners and shareholders creamed off the profits that Marx felt rightly belonged to the proletariat, the workers whose labour generated this income. As far as Marx was concerned, there was no such thing as 'good greed'. Greed was purely a case of exploiting vulnerable others for your own gain, a form of theft, and laissez-faire capitalism was designed to take the utmost advantage of that vulnerability. Marx adopted the strongest possible moral line on this issue, refusing to believe that greed could somehow or other be harnessed for the public good. Instead, in his projected social system greed was to be denied the opportunity to express itself; the collective will would triumph over that of the individual. From Smith's perspective, however, for central authority to exert total control over the economy in such a manner would amount to a condition of monopoly.

Marx was confident that the proletariat would rally to the cause of a system where wealth was to be used solely for the public good, and that capitalism would crumble when its contradictions became obvious to all: it was an inherently unfair system inimical to the interests of humanity at large. Communism, on the other hand, was to be based on cooperation, not the ruthless competition that was the norm of the capitalist market and which led to the gross inequalities Marx could see all around him in Victorian society. Marx firmly believed that economic competition could eventually be removed from human society, and saw greed as a rogue human trait that served the purposes of only a few; in his view, this meant that it could be overcome by the far superior forces of the working classes if they could be persuaded to put their mind to the task. The anarchist thinker Pierre-Joseph Proudhon argued that 'property was robbery', and although he was very critical of Proudhon's ideas (regarding anarchism as politically naive), Marx took a very similar view regarding the fruits of human labour.[12] He believed that industrialists, as a prime example, were effectively stealing the bulk of the profits accrued from labour in their factories, their workforce's 'surplus labour'. By bringing the ownership of such industries under public control, then greed too could be checked, and the fruits of surplus labour would be put to general use. As *The*

Communist Manifesto puts it: 'In place of the old bourgeois society, with its classes and class antagonisms, we shall have an association, in which the free development of each is the condition for the free development of all.'[13]

If the means of production could be made to benefit all equally, then Marx felt that we would enter something of a utopian state, with every individual set free to engage in a range of activities that he or she enjoyed, rather than being little more than servants of machines and an unfair socioeconomic system:

> As soon as the distribution of labour comes into being, each man has a particular, exclusive sphere of activity, which is forced upon him and from which he cannot escape. He is a hunter, a fisherman, a shepherd, or a critical critic, and must remain so if he does not want to lose his means of livelihood; while in communist society, where nobody has one exclusive sphere of activity but each can become accomplished in any branch he wishes, society regulates the general production and thus makes it possible for me to do one thing today and another tomorrow, to hunt in the morning, fish in the afternoon, rear cattle in the evening, criticise after dinner, just as I have a mind.[14]

Greed, to Marx, was unmistakably a moral issue. The greed of the few was leading to the misery of the vast mass of the population – the proletariat that was being exploited mercilessly by a ruthless capitalist class, which regarded them as little more than units of labour. For Marx one of the saddest aspects of this state of affairs was that it was preventing people from realizing their full potential as individuals; almost as if they were being infantilized by the capitalist system, actively discouraged from developing past a certain level.

In practice, communism was to fall far short of Marx's ideals, failing to bring an end to international capitalism and only managing to suppress greed by totalitarian means. It is instructive to consider what has happened in communism's immediate aftermath in Russia, with a small group of individuals having contrived, often by very dubious means, to gain control of the bulk of the country's rich store of natural resources, which were formerly held in public ownership (if not used very efficiently, admittedly). The oligarchs who have emerged from the Soviet system's collapse since the 1980s have exhibited enormous greed in the fortunes they have rapidly built up, leaving Russia as one of the most polarized countries in the world in terms of the distribution of its wealth. Neither do the oligarchs feed much of their wealth back into their home economy, preferring to invest their fortunes elsewhere in Europe and often living outside the country too (London has become a popular destination for Russian billionaires). The situation that now prevails in Russia is a parody of what Marx thought communism could achieve. Greed for money, property and ownership is more deeply embedded in our character than Marx thought, and it shows the ability to resurface whenever the opportunity to do so arises, no matter how suppressed it may have been beforehand. Seventy years of communism failed to remove greed from the human psyche in this case; the existence of a black market throughout Soviet times indicates that this never really went away, all the state's propaganda notwithstanding.

Nor have decades of communist rule in China been much more successful in altering human psychology. There, the Communist Party now permits capitalist enterprise to operate – if under close government supervision – in a bid to stimulate the economic growth needed to raise the living standards of the world's largest population: 'state capitalism', as its detractors on the left dismissively refer to the system. Communist economics was signally failing to deliver such an improvement, never mind the utopian conditions that Marx had predicted it would once implemented. The country is now closely tied into the global economic system, having transformed itself into the world's second largest economy in just a few decades of explosive growth. Granted, this was from a very low starting point in terms of the average standard of living, but the annual increases in the GDP were quite astonishing all the same (maintaining that growth is becoming something of an issue, however). As in Russia, this has resulted in a rapidly growing discrepancy between rich and poor, for all that the Communist Party exercises ultimate control over the nation's economic life. Marx would hardly have approved of this either; for him the point of communism was to level out economic disparity, and to abolish the greed that generated it in the first place. None of the communist regimes the world has seen have ever managed to achieve that feat, and it was a critical factor in the implosion of the Soviet bloc in the 1980s, as it became ever more apparent even to the Communist Party hierarchy just how far it was falling behind the West in economic terms.

Despite the abject failure of Marxist economics in the Soviet bloc and China (and it is worth remembering that it was a large-scale experiment involving around a quarter of the world's population at its height), Marx is still to be given credit for his undoubted talent as an analyst of capitalism, homing in unerringly on its weak points and contradictions. We are still living with those weaknesses today, and if anything neoliberal economics and globalization have made these progressively more obvious. Discrepancies in wealth, both within the world's leading economies and between them and those of the developing world, are magnifying, and it seems clear that the system is urgently in need of reform (even if the Marxist solution can now be discounted, given its distinctly poor performance record). What Marx's researches reveal is that capitalism is a system essentially based on greed: the greed of an elite able to manipulate a nation's economic life to its own ends. What he did not foresee, however, was just how much support for the system there could be outside that elite; the degree to which capitalism appealed to self-interest, such that even those who recognized the contradictions it involved nevertheless would go along with it to see where it might take them individually. Capitalism's appeal is that it offers the chance to improve oneself economically, if things work out right. It may not be all that rational to believe that they will, that we can manage to play the system to our advantage and succeed where most others do not, but human beings are probably a lot less rational in their everyday lives than a philosopher like Marx chose to believe (no one would ever play the lottery otherwise). Philosophers often make this mistake, but it should be noted that market enthusiasts like neoliberals are just as culpable in their belief that investors essentially act from rational premises, carefully calculating the state of the market before making any investment. The herd-like behaviour that creates both booms and busts would definitely cast severe doubt on that notion. These more often appear to feature outright hysteria than calm, rational decision-making. Market equilibrium is something of a pipe-dream.

Smith certainly did pick up on the importance of self-interest in human affairs, hence his support for a system that actively fostered it at every turn, and it is his vision that holds throughout the world's leading economies today. This is the case even in China, with its rising class of rich manufacturers and traders, as permitted by the new economic order there. Where Smith is to be questioned, and neoliberalism is at its most contradictory in the face of evidence to the contrary, is in his belief that the 'invisible hand' will always work to the general public advantage. If it did, then we should not be experiencing the kind of roller-coasting economics that have increasingly been the norm in the past few decades, where greed is the rogue element that can knock the system seriously out of kilter. As Stiglitz insisted, competition is anything but 'automatically perfect'. Smith's point that self-interest doesn't see (or even concern itself) with the wider picture can be interpreted in a much more negative way than he intended. Self-interest may not care what happens to the system as long as it gets its own way; indeed, it may keep going even if it is fully aware that it is manifestly not in society's best interests for it to do so. The 'invisible hand' can work against the public good just as easily as it can for it, and Smith is possibly being too idealistic in regarding it as an essentially positive force. To reject Marx does not mean that Smith has all the answers on how to run an economy, or that his view of how it works is not just as flawed in its way; self-interest is not the economic panacea he envisaged it to be. Neither is competition an unqualified good, not when it is capable of being as socially divisive as it has of late. Both the red corner and the blue corner are therefore guilty of idealism, plus a large dollop of wishful thinking, and the economy remains a matter of some considerable contention.

Businesses are well capable of displaying self-interest in terms of their working practices, as has been coming to light for some years now with regard to the restaurant and catering industry. Tipping the waiting staff after a meal out is a long-established habit around the world, almost an automatic response among diners; but the British public has been somewhat shocked to find out what is actually happening to their tips in some establishments, especially where a service charge is automatically added to the bill. Unbeknownst to the customer, the restaurant management has often been taking a cut of tips or service charges, levying a certain percentage (sometimes quite substantial) for processing the tips and then passing what is left back to the staff. A campaign has been mounted against this practice, and it has had an effect on some high-profile cases – major restaurant chains, for example, some of whom have now renounced the practice in response to the bad publicity it was generating. Since staff in the industry are generally paid very low wages in the first place, keeping back any of the tips the public thought was going to waiting staff to top up their earnings can seem very mean – an underhanded way of increasing the company's profits at the expense of its employees. Some companies had even been paying less than the minimum wage, on the understanding that whatever was being received in tips would make up the difference. Those with the most money are taking from those with the least, a situation that well merits the description of greed.

It is also greed that lies behind tax avoidance, which is all too common among the higher earners in Western societies, who tend to be staunch advocates of the free market system. Belief in the free market in this instance is interpreted to mean the right to shop around as to what system offers the best deal for your personal tax liability. While it might just be possible to understand this practice if it was occurring at the lower end of the socio-economic scale, where many are struggling to make ends meet on low wages, it is much more difficult to do so when the people in question are pulling in very high salaries at the upper end. The fact that there are loopholes in the law enabling the practice to exist, enables sharp accountants – not a service that those at the lower end economically could ever afford to call upon, or who would want their custom anyway – to take advantage of these on behalf of their well-off clients. No one making use of this system is in any financial need of extra money; they simply want to be even richer than they plainly are, treating tax as a personal imposition rather than a social obligation. In their view, the government is taking away money that is rightly theirs, and they only talk about the amount they are taxed, not what is left over after that tax is deducted, which to the average wage-earner is invariably still a huge sum of money. Neoliberalism has fostered such an outlook, tending to argue that tax of any kind is an evil, and refusing to acknowledge that taxation is one of the foundations of a civilized society. This point is vigorously argued by Richard Murphy in his book *The Joy of Tax* (2015), and even if his ideas about how to reform the tax system to ensure greater fairness, and revenues for governments to work with, will be controversial (among higher earners, certainly), the underlying notion of tax's value to society is sound. For all that tax can, as Murphy notes, arouse 'resentment' in those levied, we need to keep reminding ourselves that without the revenue it yields governments could barely function at all.[15]

Taxation has been cut quite substantially in the UK in the last two to three decades, and all the country's income tax bands are now set much lower than they were in the immediate post-war years when the welfare system was being radically expanded. In fact, there has been a general trend throughout the West in recent years to bring income tax down, as well as to head towards similar reductions in the future. Most mainstream political parties regard it as electoral poison to campaign for higher taxes. Nevertheless, neoliberals still complain that they are too high, and campaign to have them lowered still further. Such attitudes help to create a culture where tax avoidance can seem a perfectly reasonable step to take, and those with the wherewithal turn to their accountants to arrange what they can. The lower the income tax rate drops, the more public sector cuts we experience, but these barely impact on higher earners anyway – especially those with enough wealth to make tax avoidance schemes seem like worthwhile propositions. Thomas Piketty has warned that if we go on in this way, 'there is a serious risk that the very notion of fiscal consent – which is at the core of modern democracies – will fall apart altogether'.[16]

Greed is the obvious way of describing the motives involved in tax avoidance: wanting more purely for the sake of it. Once again, social conscience, and the commitment to fiscal consent it ought to induce in any reasonable individual, appears to be most notable by its absence. If you are earning several times the average salary (sometimes several hundred times), then why should you not pay the same tax as a group of individuals whose collective earnings are the same as yours? Social justice would dictate that you should – at least as a minimum requirement. Economists like Piketty argue that higher earners should be paying more, as a step towards reducing discrepancies in wealth and boosting egalitarianism. Yet the lure of more money seems to erode the individual's sense of social responsibility rather too frequently.

The moral side of what is happening is very problematic. Some members of the public are clearly receiving preferential treatment that is only accessible to those with lots of money. Self-interest is running riot, apparently with official sanction.

Western governments periodically make promises to curtail this system when some particularly glaring example happens to spark a public outcry, but they also put forward several arguments to defend maintaining some measure of flexibility within the tax regime. We are warned that the rich might leave the country if they are denied the opportunity to make use of such schemes, and almost any suggestion that tax rises are being considered by the government immediately generates headlines in the right-wing press with just that threat being made. We are also reminded that the world is full of tax havens which would be only too willing to take such tax exiles in, as they do on a regular basis, and that multinational corporations would be at the forefront of the exodus. Most of us would see this as a reason for cracking down on tax havens – which might more properly be called 'tax-evasion zones'. Periodic promises by governments to do so are, however, usually honoured in the breach, with the right noises being made but little substantive action following on from these. Neoliberal economics and the globalization ethic are committed to the free movement of capital around the globe, and this works against restrictions on low-tax regimes where capital can yield more gain – exactly what capitalism is always aiming to achieve. The international financial system that is in place is therefore effectively promoting a culture of tax avoidance, which is also to say, encouraging a culture of greed.

As noted, multinationals make extensive use of this system to avoid paying taxes in many of the countries they are operating within – and very profitably too. One such haven, Bermuda, levies corporation tax at the princely rate of 0 per cent. Others allow companies to be registered as being based there for a mere pittance (British Virgin Islands, for example, among many others), turning them into very attractive locations for calculating multinationals to claim as their headquarters. Several cases of this have come to light in the UK of late, where it has been brought to the public's attention that many large companies trading throughout the country are paying little tax, or often no tax at all (and the UK is not alone in this respect; this is an international problem). In a recent report, for example, Facebook was cited as paying less tax in the UK than an individual UK taxpayer – only a few thousand pounds, shamefully enough. The companies in question may trade here, but they are not based here, choosing instead to channel their profits back to their headquarters, conveniently situated in lower-tax locations, a practice that has been described as 'profit shifting'.[17] The fact that said companies are worth billions, and would have little difficulty in meeting the tax requirements of countries such as the UK and accepting lower returns, makes what is happening even more deplorable. Sometimes it can feel as if the only people actually paying tax are those in the standard tax brackets; corporations increasingly seem able to find ways round that liability. Smith's 'universal competition' does not seem to generate a 'universal sense of social responsibility'. Owners and shareholders are reaping the benefits that, morally at least, ought to be going to the public purse in order to maintain the kind of infrastructure that companies require to trade within. At times like this, there really does seem to be one law for the rich and one for the poor.

It is a system that is gaining the attention of a group of economists who are concerned at the implications it has for public finances – an issue of some importance in an era of austerity. One such economist is Gabriel Zucman, whose book *The Hidden Wealth of Nations: The Scourge of Tax Havens* (2015), takes a very dim view of how multinationals have been abusing the system for some time now. He puts forward some very practical solutions as to ways by which the system could be reformed to recover this growing cache of 'hidden wealth' for more general use, stating uncompromisingly that tax havens 'steal the revenue of foreign nations'.[18] Unfortunately Zucman's 'action plan' for recovering this lost revenue would require international cooperation on a scale that does not appear to be forthcoming at present; there are simply too many vested interests involved, all well versed in defending their corner. Overcoming that resistance will take more than the presentation of eminently sensible suggestions, such as the creation of a 'global financial register' with the task of 'recording who owns all the financial securities in circulation, stocks, bonds, and shares of mutual funds throughout the world', on the grounds that this would constitute 'a concrete embodiment of the notion of financial transparency'.[19] Nevertheless, as long as economists like Zucman are drawing attention to the problem, then the harder it will become for governments to continue to turn a blind eye to it, as has been the pattern for far too long. Zucman is correct in arguing that at some point the issue has to be faced, politically messy and awkward though it will undoubtedly be.

There may be no necessary connection between tax avoidance and free market economics (some of the rich do abide by the rules in their country of residence and dutifully pay their taxes), but the laissez-faire ethos does set a certain kind of tone in which self-interest seems to thrive to an unhealthy degree. I doubt if this is what Adam Smith would have wanted either; he is more likely to have identified an ethical breach taking place in such cases. Yet once self-interest is given its head then it becomes difficult to prevent it from pushing to the extremes that we are currently experiencing – and tax avoidance is only one of several antisocial consequences that ensue. In Zucman's uncompromising words: 'It's important to understand that we're not talking about tax competition, but of theft pure and simple: Switzerland, Luxembourg, or the Cayman Islands offer some taxpayers who wish to do so the possibility of stealing from their governments.'[20] If it is theft that we are ultimately dealing with, theft stemming from the overweening greed of everyone connected to such an unsavoury practice, then governments should be duty-bound to take preventative action on behalf of the public. Neoliberals think the theft is occurring in the other direction, however, meaning there is a considerable difference of opinion over this issue.

While not technically tax evasion, philanthropy can also reduce one's tax bill, since it is generally eligible for tax relief, and a new wave of so called 'philanthrocapitalists' have been known to view it in just that way, as the sociologist Linsey McGoey points out in her book *No Such Thing as a Free Gift* (2015).[21] As the title suggests, McGoey is deeply suspicious of the motives behind philanthro-capitalism, querying whether it might be merely an excuse to widen the sphere of operations of the economics of greed. From that perspective, charitable giving is just another business, and one ripe for a take-over. Those engaged in the activity cannot envisage any area of human endeavour in which neoliberal principles do not apply, or that could not be improved by the adoption of market methods; hence their tendency to be quite ruthless in their approach to philanthropy, pulling out of any scheme their foundation has started if they do not think it is achieving the success for which they have been aiming. Yet another form of greed is in evidence here, and that is greed for fame. Philanthropy generally attracts good publicity and can give a gloss to your reputation; thus any tax you save also contributes towards improving your public image. To a highly successful entrepreneur, this will seem an altogether better bargain than seeing the money disappear into the public purse, a trade-off worth accessing. In effect, they are buying a better image for themselves; it is just another transaction. Turning charity into a mere product does, however, seem to be sinking to a new low.

The economics of greed can also be found at work in organized religion. In the U.S. there is certainly a free market in that field among the televangelical community, who vie with each other for the biggest share of the audience, and the money this can bring along with it. The rewards can be very high for achieving popularity, justifying vigorous competition among theological peers. Most religions apply any earnings they may have towards good works of one kind or another, but televangelism is a fully fledged commercial industry, which can deliver a glamorous lifestyle for its practitioners – that is an expected part of the package. Televangelists make unashamed use of market principles, selling a wide range of goods to build up substantial fortunes for their churches and for themselves as the business brains behind the enterprise. Donations are another considerable source of revenue, with the television format providing ample scope for soliciting these from viewers, often using typically American hard-sell tactics to drive the message home.

We might think that parading one's riches goes against the spirit of religion, which ostensibly has no place for pride and avarice, both deemed 'deadly sins'. Yet conspicuous consumption is almost a badge of office among televangelists, which also runs the risk of inducing in their audience feelings of covetousness, and that is outlawed in the Ten Commandments – a further twist of religious doctrine. Instead, for televangelists, and much of their audience too, economic success is interpreted as a marker of divine approval (admittedly Protestantism has a long, and not particularly proud, history of making that connection).[22] In this context, presenting an image of being wealthy therefore sends out the right message, indicating that God is on your side. God is just one more product to be sold on the open market, and in a nation as committed to business as the U.S., that can seem quite natural. Laissez-faire capitalism is as applicable to religion as anything else, and a significant proportion of the American public is a firm believer in both, seeing no clash of values involved.

Laissez-faire economics are increasingly being applied to the field of education too, with higher education becoming an area of considerable interest to the private sector. In Western Europe in the modern era higher education has generally been a publicly funded exercise, with the state assuming responsibility for maintaining the university system on the basis that education is a public good. Of late, however, many governments, including that of the UK, have been encouraging the establishment of private universities, and these have been springing up, based firmly on 'for-profit' principles. Predictably, such institutions tend to follow the money, concentrating on subjects for which there is a proven large market. Business studies is a particular favourite, given that it is so obviously career-oriented (MBAs are among the most sought-after degrees in the world at present), and it is also fairly low-cost to run. In the main, private higher education compares very poorly with public sector provision; but to governments of a neoliberal persuasion it represents a way of saving public money and being able to promise yet lower taxes in future if the system grows substantially enough, drawing demand away from the public sector as it does so. The private sector makes the expected noises about helping to extend choice and bringing greater diversity to educational provision, but their real interest is in exploiting yet another potential source of profit. Providing a public service is not why they are attracted to the enterprise; it is simply another business opportunity, and they will run it with an eye to profit first and foremost.

In the public sector, meanwhile, the same phenomenon of a growing discrepancy between those at the top and bottom of the salary scale is well under way. Vice-chancellors in UK universities have seen their pay soar in recent years, while those in the lower reaches of the lecturer scale have seen theirs remaining, at best, stagnant, thus falling in real terms. Coupled with this has been a marked shift towards part-time, hourly paid work among teaching staff as government funding to the sector is significantly reduced. This is a policy in line with neoliberal principles to keep government and public funding out of the employment market as much as possible, and bring about greater 'flexibility' – a concept that suits management but by no means the rest of the workforce. Whereas young academics could once treat this system as a way into the profession on a full-time basis (as I did myself in my early career), now many are finding themselves stuck indefinitely on short-term, part-time contracts with no guarantee of renewal each time around. Casualization is now the order of the day in higher education, and likely to get worse before it gets better. The situation is even more desperate in the American academic world, where it has been reported that as many as 76 per cent of academics are on casual contracts, effectively cut off from any real chance of permanent appointment and financial security. What was once a minority is now a majority – and becoming steadily larger. This is a recognizable trend throughout the whole world of employment, and those at the top end are cashing in on it quite unashamedly, 'selfish passions' well to the fore as outgoings on employee wages are slashed. Flexibility can be profitable for some. The flow of wealth is dramatically one-way, and it is fuelling ever more greed, with demand continuing to exceed need at every stage.

The blue corner has, it seems, defeated the red corner, and apparently comprehensively. Wherever we are on the political spectrum, we shall have to accommodate ourselves to that, although that need not mean that we surrender to it and accept its excesses as simply the way of the world. The question is whether it can be held in check from within. The criticisms of those such as Stiglitz, Piketty and Zucman suggest that reform of the system is now firmly on the agenda, even if it still has some way to go to persuade the political class to face up to the insatiable greed of the neoliberal financial empire. It is, however, a step in the right direction.

4

A WORLD FIT FOR SHAREHOLDERS: GREED AND THE FINANCIAL INDUSTRY

Perhaps the financial sector really is full of predatory figures like Gordon Gekko, but they would rarely express themselves that way, being well aware of the public opprobrium it would undoubtedly generate if, like Sherman McCoy, they were ever to claim to merit the title of 'Masters of the Universe'. 'Selfish passions' of that nature normally remain unvoiced – except among the initiated, and away from the public gaze. Instead, the rationale for the system has increasingly been shifted over to shareholders, who are used to justify almost any action by corporations that pushes up profits. These actions include using tax havens, issuing zero-hours contracts and using agencies to supply the workforce as needed on a casual basis so that responsibility for fringe benefits such as pension contributions and holiday pay can be avoided. While some people actually want employment on a casual or flexible basis, an increasing number are being pushed into it because it is being adopted as policy in both the public and private sectors as a way to cut the wages bill. What might be called the 'shareholder defence' is now a standard tactic of neoliberal theorists, used as justification for the economics of greed that drives the stock market relentlessly on, without much regard for the social effect. The rights of shareholders seemingly have to be protected at all costs, and the system uses all its political acumen to keep itself as free as possible from any outside interference.

What are those rights that appear to sanction the continuing rise of the greedocracy? Milton Friedman, the doyen of monetarism (which sparked off neoliberal economics), argued forcefully that a company's primary responsibility was to its shareholders, and that it should as a matter of principle put their interests ahead of those of the general public. He went so far as to claim that it would be immoral of any company to do otherwise.[1] Anything that reduced shareholders' returns on their investment in any way represented a serious dereliction of duty on the company's part – an argument that could hardly be further away from Marx's conception of morality. What the shareholder wants, the shareholder should get; and what the shareholder obviously wanted was higher dividends – that was their right. At least that was the assumption made by theorists of the Friedman ilk. The principle applies no matter what the company is selling, even if it is healthcare or education. Whatever form they take, products exist in order to make profits for whoever is selling them, and that principle is not to be breached. They may be useful, or they may not, but as long as they are bought then the producer need not really care. Commercial enterprises do not engage in business for the public good; if that happens to come about then it is merely a side effect of the pursuit of profit. There has been an issue in the UK recently over companies, in several areas of commercial activity, cutting back on spending on health and safety requirements – an example of what the profit principle can lead to in action. Health and safety do require a certain amount of outlay after all, which otherwise would flow towards shareholders. It takes a serious accident, and the media interest that inevitably attracts, to bring attention to any cutbacks in this area, and to make any company found guilty of negligence start to take their responsibilities seriously. Even when they do, it is probably as much to repair their public image as anything to do with an ideological turnaround on their part; profit margins will always be in the forefront of their thinking.

Neoliberal economics believes that the public interest is best served by corporations pursuing the largest possible dividends for their shareholders, in that this will spur the economy on to greater heights and thus generate faster growth – which then feeds back far more to management and shareholders than it does to the general public. Opponents, however, have countered with the 'stakeholder defence', arguing that everyone has a stake in the economy and not just shareholders, who form only a minority of the population and have their own individual agendas. The contention is that there have to be stakeholder rights as well if we are to have a fair society. From the stakeholder perspective, what is best for shareholders is not necessarily best for society in general, the vast body of stakeholders. In fact, in many cases society needs to be protected from shareholders, a qualification that clearly applies in the reference above to health and safety issues. Politically, this is a difficult balancing act that has been made all the more awkward by the widespread adoption of neoliberal policies around the globe in recent times. Neither is neoliberalism a system that is easy to opt out of or ignore, given the enthusiasm shown for it by the world's leading economies, the ones who set the terms for global trade. If you engage in any kind of business at all on the international market, and most economies are crucially dependent on this activity, then you will be drawn into a neoliberal network that will determine the conditions of trading; at present, there is no way of escaping that.

Stakeholders are very much on the sidelines in a world where multinationals can wield so much economic power, plus the political influence that naturally follows on from that. Governments are always very wary of upsetting multinationals, since both jobs and a nation's gross domestic product (GDP) are so dependent on their operations. The fact that so many of those corporations manage to avoid paying their share of national taxes – often none at all, despite running extensive operations in various European nations – indicates the scale of influence that they can wield. The failure of so many governments to close the loopholes that allow this practice to flourish, such as the continued existence of tax havens and offshore banking, also speaks volumes. Tax havens are turning into the corporate world's best friend, places that enable them to beat the system that applies to stakeholders in the world's major economies. Increasingly it is the case that the tax burden is being borne by stakeholders rather than corporations, and this is beginning to generate protest among the former group, as the implications of this trend come to sink in; the major implication being that the wealth gap is becoming ever wider. Shareholders versus stockholders is another debate that rumbles on, although the latter are undoubtedly in the ascendancy under the current neoliberal regime, where the market is privileged to such a socially unhealthy degree. The rights of the shareholder trump the rights of the stakeholder in this system. Smith's 'invisible hand' clearly helps some much more than it does others.

The 'shareholder defence' is based on the premise that anything that might reduce a company's annual profits amounts to taking it away from shareholders. Substantially increasing wage levels for its workers (except top management, that is, who are very careful to protect themselves on that score), or supporting worthy public causes financially, would have that undesirable effect, so are to be resisted. This is a very different kind of economic 'theft' than the one Marx was railing about: possessive individualism rules in this area. Companies are held to exist almost solely for the purpose of maximizing profit margins, and that is assumed to be why shareholders invest in them in the first place. Social conscience is considered to be a purely private matter, something individuals display, using their own money (which they are free to dispose of as they wish), not commercial organizations. Nor do neoliberals regard this as greed; to them it is simply realistic business practice, and they expect to find nothing less applying in the commercial sector at all times. Charity begins at home, not at work – and certainly not in the shareholder's name.

We are entitled to ask just what it is about being a shareholder that appears to grant people such a privileged position in the current world economic order. How did we end up in this position?

In effect, shareholders have become the 'invisible hand', with the depth of their investment in a corporation dictating its share price and the movement of the market. It has to be remembered, too, that stock market flotations can be very profitable events, so companies want to look as attractive as possible to prospective shareholders. If a share price goes up then it will become more interesting to the investor community. Greed knows no loyalty in that respect; it follows success, and that is what a rising share price strongly implies, pulling in investment with it – as well as making further market flotations seem possible. A surge of investors will invariably affect the price of other stocks, often driving down those of the corporation's main competitors – precisely what every corporation is trying so keenly to achieve. If, on the other hand, a share price goes down substantially, then it is very likely that investors will start to shift their investment elsewhere, always chasing higher dividends. That is the whole point of investing, plain and simple. Market ups and downs are what give shareholders the power they have, and explain why corporations are so intent on maximizing their dividends.

No doubt some shareholders are as single-minded about their investments as the assumption has it, concerned solely with the size of dividends rather than any matters of social conscience. That is certainly what Friedman believes, and neoliberal economists in general: their theories are dedicated to making this a world fit for shareholders. Other shareholders, however, may lay more emphasis on benefit to society than profit – those who seek out 'ethical investments', for example, such as any that are ecoconscious or 'fair trade' (for all the problems that can arise with these categories). This offers the possibility that if there were enough ethically concerned shareholders in a company, they could have a significant impact on company policy. Shareholders could, in theory, rally together at annual general meetings and demand that the company they were investing in act more ethically in future. This would be a very practical way of reforming the system from within. In a recent example of such a situation shareholders of BP and Smith & Nephew voted against large increases in pay to their company's chief executives at general meetings in 2016. In 2012 there was an even more widespread rebellion about executive pay deals in what the media dubbed the 'Shareholder Spring'. Executive bonuses have grown out of all proportion to average wages, and have created an ongoing public scandal, with the banking industry being particularly culpable. There is, after all, persuasive evidence to suggest that the rich are taking an ever larger share of the national wealth throughout Western societies, and that stakeholders are in consequence falling further and further behind. Thomas Piketty's work provides comprehensive statistical back-up to substantiate this.

One might assume that a shareholder revolt could arrest the practice, forcing bonuses down and insisting that the company in question acts in a more socially responsible manner. Sometimes even a stakeholder revolt can have that effect. A public campaign against bankers' bonuses in the Netherlands in 2011, for example, persuaded the Dutch government to pass a law banning these bonuses in banks that had received a public bailout; surely a completely reasonable policy under the circumstances.[2] Yet while several shareholder revolts have occurred in the UK in the last few years, they have rarely seemed to have had all that much impact, other than some bad publicity in the media, which soon dies away (reports are usually consigned to the business news section anyway, which rarely reaches the attention of most of the wider public). Companies generally agree to re-examine their wage structure at executive level, but rarely make any significant changes. One could be cynical and wonder if shareholders who revolt are possibly at least as interested in increasing their own share dividends by diverting bonuses their own way, to be split among them. This would be entirely in line with Friedmanite doctrine; so perhaps this is greed in operation yet again. Or might it be that shareholders are mainly worried that widespread adverse public reaction over the bonus system, such as moving their custom elsewhere in protest, could put the company's profits at risk? In this case, shareholders might merely be trying to protect their investment, which is dependent on the company's good reputation. The financial industry very much encourages such scepticism on the part of onlookers. Purity of motive is not a hallmark of its financial operations; everyone involved is there first and foremost for the money.

It is an assumption of neoliberal economics that what benefits the stock market also benefits society and its myriad stakeholders. While this may be true on longer timescales (standards of living are clearly much higher on average in the West than they were, say, a century ago, and a market-based economy has played a part in that achievement), it is more debatable in the shorter term. We are now living in a period where living standards are actually declining for a significant proportion of the population, and often quite sharply. Members of the younger generation in particular find themselves facing a much bleaker economic outlook than their parents did, with radically diminished career prospects. This is the pattern not just in the UK and Western Europe, but in the U.S., as Piketty's *Capital in the Twenty-first Century* goes into such detail to prove:

> The top decile claimed as much as 45–50 percent of national income in the 1910s–1920s before dropping to 30–35 percent by the end of the 1940s. Inequality then stabilized at that level from 1950 to 1970. We subsequently see a rapid rise in inequality in the 1980s, until by 2000 we have returned to a level on the order of 45–50 percent of national income. The magnitude of the change is impressive.[3]

If this discrepancy between rich and poor continues to get wider, as it has done for quite some time now, then it would raise very serious doubts about the validity of neoliberal economics, since the recent rise in inequality post-1980s coincides with the widespread adoption of neoliberal policies. Greed appears to be reasserting itself, and strongly, after a brief period of losing its dominance. One of the most depressing features of Piketty's researches is how they reveal that greed's domination is the norm, and that is not good news for democracy. The mid-century, post-war spike in wages and relative wealth is the exception rather than the rule in modern times, and that is a sobering thought. Societies are having to face the distinct likelihood of each generation being poorer than its predecessor, which is not the message our political class has been trained to deliver, or the electorate to expect.

Economists like Piketty are already beginning to ask probing questions about neoliberalism's stranglehold on the world economy. Noting that 'The distribution of wealth is one of today's most widely discussed and controversial issues,' Piketty's response is to call for government action to reduce the wealth gap in Western societies.[4] Only by taxing the very wealthy on their capital, he maintains, can we hope to reverse this discrepancy and move towards a more just society for stakeholders. He suggests a 'wealth tax' that could be set at '10 percent or higher on billionaires', precisely the group most likely to be engaging in tax avoidance schemes, as well as the group most likely to be able to exert behind-the-scenes pressure on governments to prevent such a tax from ever being levied.[5] Were this ever to come to pass, however, it would be an economically healthier society overall in Piketty's opinion, and less prone to sudden booms and busts, given that the greed impulse would have its scope for operation restricted.

We cannot rely on the market alone to bring about this desirable state of affairs; that is just not the way the system works, as we know from long, and frequently bitter, experience. This situation requires urgent attention if the level of consensus required to operate a democratic society is to be maintained. As both Piketty and Zucman point out, 'fiscal consent' is already under a great deal of strain from the tax haven system, since it implies that tax is only for the poorest to middle-income groups, and suggests that the wealthy are not pulling their weight in terms of social responsibility. Anger at this would be an understandable reaction, since it is demonstrably unfair, and bringing in a 10 per cent tax on fortunes would therefore seem to be an eminently defensible policy to adopt.

The role played by greed in the growing global disparity between rich and poor has not gone unnoticed by the general public, however, and a resistance to it has been building up gradually in recent years. An anti-capitalist movement has developed, which makes itself very visible – and generates substantial media coverage – by holding protests at international governmental conferences such as G8 summits (now heavily policed as a consequence), with demonstrators brandishing placards with provocative slogans such as 'Greed Kills'. The Occupy Wall Street protest struck a chord with the general public, and other Occupy movements have been active throughout the world (in the City of London, for example), generating a considerable degree of popular support and sympathy for their ideals. The credit crash has brought home to the general public just how vulnerable we are to a financial system where greed is such a central factor. Whether or not 'greed kills', it most certainly does drive down average earnings (as well as employment security) in the stakeholder constituency. It is greed that is widening the disparity in wealth between the rich 1 per cent (the ones Piketty's wealth tax is designed to target) and the rest of society, and this widening gap is becoming one of the most critical cultural problems of our time. It is an unhealthy social situation all round, as even some of the 1 per cent themselves acknowledge, and it has led to an interesting phenomenon: the emergence of wealth therapy for the mega-rich.

Marx would have been appalled at the idea of providing therapy for those who feel guilty about their financial success and are upset by the vocal public opposition it is now drawing – perhaps even Adam Smith would have been, too. Yet wealth therapy has become an actual field (originating, entirely predictably, in the United States), and its practitioners are insistent that we should be more sympathetic to the psychological problems that excessive wealth can cause to sensitive individuals. There is even a foundation called the Wealth Legacy Group, which exists to speak out publicly on behalf of what proponents argue is fast becoming a demonized section of the population. The group's founder, Jamie Traeger-Muney, condemns the fact that movements like Occupy are 'making a value judgment about a particular group of people', that is, unfairly turning them into scapegoats for the failures of the financial system.[6] The consequences of this, Traeger-Muney says, are that the very wealthy are effectively becoming social outcasts who are unable to mix freely with others. He further dramatizes the current plight of the rich, especially the super-rich, by asserting that 'Coming out to people about their wealth is similar to coming out of the closet as gay' (one has to wonder what the gay community would make of such a comparison).[7]

The argument behind such comments is that no one individual is personally responsible for the wealth gap, so should not be made to feel guilty about its existence. This is a fair enough point in its way, and scapegoating is not an attractive social trait – something that immigrants and refugees, and those receiving welfare benefits, know only too well these days. Yet it does suggest a lack of understanding about just how bad it can feel to be at the lower end of the socioeconomic scale in an era when public spending is being savagely cut again and again and wages are falling – with welfare schemes being at the sharp end of such cutbacks, thus exacerbating the situation – and when the cuts are made in response to a financial crisis that appears to have left those at the upper end of the scale largely unaffected. Oxfam has produced figures that claim the 1 per cent's share of global wealth rose from 44 per cent to 48 per cent in the period 2009–14 – in the aftermath of the credit crash. When such figures are examined together with the researches of both Piketty and Zucman, a definite pattern begins to emerge. In 2010 the UK's incoming coalition government insisted that we had to recognize that 'we are all in this together', but this has proved to be an empty claim. There is a section of the population that plainly isn't 'in this' with everyone else, but is in fact cashing in on the crisis quite nicely and remains untouched by the public sector cuts that the principle of mutual responsibility has repeatedly been used to justify. Perhaps the super-rich ought to reflect more seriously on their situation in a time of widespread economic disorder, rather than consulting wealth therapists?

For Piketty, then, it will only be when Western governments introduce substantial tax increases for society's higher earners that the current drift towards greater and greater disparity, and a further decline in the standard of living for the vast majority of the population, will be arrested. This is a seductively simple solution, as well as bad news for wealth therapists everywhere, but it does have its drawbacks. Popular though the idea of a wealth tax might well be among the stakeholder section of society, it would be anything but among the rich, and the statistics on tax evasion do not encourage a great deal of optimism about social conscience in that class – at least in any general sense. It is proving difficult enough to get the rich to pay taxes as they currently stand, never mind what they would consider to be punitive rates that implied further demonization. Faced with higher taxes they have many options that they could exercise, and they would undoubtedly take advantage of them as rapidly as possible. For most, the experience of psychological guilt would be preferable to any substantial reduction in their wealth; fiscal consent is very weak among this group. When France introduced just such a punitive rate in 2012 (75 per cent for earnings from €1 million upwards, outdoing even Piketty's suggestions), there was something of an outcry in the country, even though polls appeared to show a majority in favour of increased taxes on the very wealthy. Several high-profile individuals (notably the film star Gérard Depardieu) left France and took up residence in other European countries that had lower tax rates, such as Belgium. So unpopular did the tax prove that the French government felt itself forced to back down, and it was repealed in early 2015. Other European governments will hardly have been inspired to follow suit by such an outcome. The era of the stakeholder is still to come.

A world fit for shareholders is a world fit for the market, and the market is not going to go away. You might take that as a counsel of despair, but we must always remember that the market is a human invention; it is not a given – like nature, say. It does give the impression of springing from something deep in human nature, but we are not fated to give in to that, to allow everything in it full expression, whatever the effect may be. If we did, then we would not be living in an ordered society of the kind that we have developed; it would be more like Hobbes's nightmare. We need a new definition of what constitutes a 'world fit for share-holders' that does not involve quite such appalling treatment of stakeholders. Milton Friedman cannot be allowed to have the last word on the subject.

Neither does a world fit for shareholders equate to a world fit for workers. Employment practices in the West are regressing, and that cannot just be put down to the current bout of austerity. Factory and shop workers are finding their conditions deteriorating as employers find new ways of contracting them that save money, thus funnelling yet more of their profits back to owners and shareholders, and swelling the ranks of what the political theorist Guy Standing has dubbed the 'precariat' class.[8] Workers' rights have been steadily eroding as market principles are applied more and more ruthlessly. In warehouses providing services for online ordering organizations, as a case in point, workers are often treated little better than robots, with their body movements monitored by gadgets such as wristbands or ankle bands to check that they are working hard enough. Some companies in this business have taken this to its logical conclusion, and are beginning to use actual robots on the warehouse floor. Trade unions have been hobbled by a series of new laws curbing their powers (to organize, to strike or to bargain) and are less able to protect their members from unscrupulous employers – that is, where unions still exist, as they have been banned in many work-places. The cumulative effect of such changes has been a dramatic fall in workplace unionization over the last few decades, which is now shrinking fast from its post-war peak.

The media has standardly taken to calling current employment practices 'Dickensian', and it often takes an investigation from a newspaper or television company before the public discovers just how bad the situation can be in some firms. Sometimes this jolts shareholders into complaining to company management and demanding improvement in working practices (although it will usually require a public outcry before shareholders do make such awkward demands), and stock market value can fall as a result of the adverse attention. Even more worrying is the underlying cast of mind this situation reveals in employers: that the workforce must be squeezed as hard as possible so that profits increase, and that management should test just how far they can push employees before outsiders notice (and they don't always notice). Given enough of a public outcry, however, even business-friendly governments can find it expedient to look into a corporation's practices. Sadly it usually takes an extreme example before that happens, and as long as companies stay on just the right side of the law they will usually get away with sharp practices on the employment front; zero-hours contracts may not be fair, but they are still legal. Only greed can explain this policy, which sounds more like Hobbes's dreaded 'state of nature' than twenty-first-century liberal democracy. Sadly this is an attitude that gives the impression of being widespread in this milieu, which is yet another damning comment on human nature: a case of prey on the vulnerable when you are in a position of power, and continue to do so unless you are caught. Meanness has become the most desirable trait for managers to display, as if corporations are out to prove that it is the mean who are destined to inherit the earth rather than the meek.

Helpful though investigative journalism can be, it cannot uncover every example of bad practice, and what is brought to light is most likely only the tip of the iceberg. Notwithstanding the occasional challenges made at annual general meetings, shareholders have been major beneficiaries of this marked cultural shift. There is also no doubt that it has exacerbated the trend towards greater discrepancy in wealth between the upper and lower echelons of society, as noted by socially conscious economists like Piketty and Zucman. The impact of greed on human relations, on overall quality of life, is sadly all too plain in such areas.

At some point, all of this will not add up any longer; cutting welfare benefits to the bone and driving down wages ever lower will mean that consumption of a wide range of products will drop. Then companies' profits will also drop, as the rich alone cannot provide the mass market that societies depend upon to generate prosperity and guarantee longer-term economic stability. (For that matter, neither can robots, and it remains to be seen how much of a problem their use as a workforce will pose for society. Robots do not pay tax either.) Left to its own devices, the market will always seek to increase profits by any means open to it, in the belief that equilibrium will eventually be reached. Sometimes it is – although invariably not before considerable pain for a host of vulnerable stakeholders until things settle down properly. Sometimes, however, it isn't, and we find ourselves confronted by a crisis that resists the return of equilibrium, a situation strongly suggested by the present state of the world economy. If that is where we are heading, or being pushed towards by the greed of the financial elite, then perhaps even shareholders will have to start wondering if there is something wrong with a system that is designed to benefit only the few. Neoliberalism and the financial industry really do have a lot to answer for.

5
FOOD, GREED AND CONSEQUENCES

When it comes to food, greediness appears to be a universal phenomenon: examples of greed can be found at any time in our history, in both poor and rich societies. Under the name of gluttony, it was classified as one of the Seven Deadly Sins by the medieval Christian Church, which considered it a far cry from the asceticism that was taken to be the mark of the truly spiritual believer. The individual was supposed to be more concerned with matters of the soul than the body, and excess was frowned upon. Despite this, the image of the fat, jolly friar was a common one, regularly mocked in the popular culture of the period: 'Lust and Gluttony had long been pre-eminent among the monastic vices; and these and other charges were levelled against the religious orders with increasing frequency during the fifteenth century.'[1] The notion of the Seven Deadly Sins may no longer carry the religious significance it once did, but we still colloquially refer to those with large appetites as gluttons, and usually with critical intent (even if this is disguised by a mocking humour; fat people easily become figures of fun in our society).[2] Think, too, of how a large appetite for wealth prompts jibes about 'fat cats'. Not everyone is greedy for food, or at least will display that greediness publicly, but many of our fellow human beings manifestly are. Deferred gratification plays no part in their consumption habits; instead they indulge themselves to the limit as often as they can – a highly visible example of excess in action.

Greed for food can seem to be a fairly benign trait; after all, it is an individual choice, an expression of free will, and in our culture individualism is actively championed. We are each deemed to be the 'owner' of our body, with the right to decide how to treat it. Food manufacturers, meanwhile, are only too glad to meet, and fuel, the demands of those making the choice to overeat. Greed is a major source of profit for the sector, which is keen to see all of us consume more, and then even more again on top of that; our waistlines are not their concern. To food manufacturers and retailers excess is a good trait, and they are out to cultivate it as much as they can. Yet there is a growing public awareness that it is in fact far more complicated than this, that there are social consequences, often very serious ones, to this form of greed. We are currently in the middle of what the medical profession is increasingly inclined to describe as an 'obesity epidemic' in the major Western countries, and this has far-reaching consequences that can affect all of us in one way or another. (It would have greater shock value to speak of a gluttony epidemic, but that would imply putting more blame on individuals than we are inclined to do these days.) Obesity definitely has a social cost.

It is worth noting that there is a certain amount of debate as to the exact point at which an individual can be classed as overweight. It is usually based on a scale known as the body mass index (BMI), which is established using a ratio of height to weight.[3] Generally the higher an individual's BMI, the higher their risk of medical issues such as heart disease, diabetes and other weight-related conditions (although it should be noted that BMI isn't a definitive diagnosis of obesity, as muscular people can have a high BMI without excess fat). Currently people are usually considered to be overweight if they have a BMI of over 25, with obesity starting at 30+, morbid obesity at 40+ and super-morbid obesity at 50+. Public health authorities have been challenged over whether the overweight category, being only slightly higher than the assumed 'normal' or 'ideal' BMI (18.5–25), really constitutes a significant problem. Even if possibly excessive, however, this caution is nevertheless under-standable, and the health risks do increase markedly the higher up the obese scale you move. The most common form of diabetes (Type 2), for example, is very largely the product of being seriously overweight, and can in many cases be arrested in its progress by significant weight loss (as long as it is conscientiously maintained).

It is no secret that obesity is bad for one's health, and health systems in the West are finding it increasingly difficult to cope with the various problems that the condition brings in its wake. With an estimated quarter of the UK adult population classed as overweight according to recent figures, and an even more worrying third of Americans (and rising in both instances), those problems are becoming ever more pronounced. Obese patients can be a significant drain on resources. An illustration of the financial implications can be identified in obesity in pregnancy, which causes particular problems for both mother and baby as well as for the medical staff called on to deal with the situation. Obese mothers require far more attention and care than the norm, and are prone to develop serious complications during childbirth. As the Director for the Confidential Enquiries into Maternal Deaths project (CEMACH) has pointed out: 'Obese pregnant women are probably at four or five times greater risk of suffering maternal death than a woman of normal weight – and the same for their babies dying.'[4] The issue is now being taken very seriously within health services in the West, generating a series of detailed studies into the various complications medical staff can expect to find in these situations, and how best to manage them to minimize the likelihood of the worst outcomes. A recent report indicates just how desperate these complications can turn out to be:

> There is a strong international evidence-base which shows
> an association between increased pre-pregnancy body mass
> index (BMI) and adverse pregnancy outcomes for both
> the mother and her child. Women with a BMI >30 kg/m

[squared] (clinically defined as obese) before pregnancy or in early pregnancy have a significantly increased risk of mortality, and comorbidities such as gestational diabetes and pre-eclampsia. Outcomes for the child also include reduced breastfeeding rates, increased risk of congenital anomaly, and neonatal mortality.[5]

As the study points out, all of this means extra work for the medical staff, and 'these additional interventions are associated with increased costs for health services compared with managing pregnancies of women within the recommended BMI range'.[6]

Extremely obese pregnant women may also be in need of special facilities during their hospital stay, adding to the increased costs. Beds and operating tables, for example, may be unable to cope with their weight, requiring specially strengthened ones to be made available for their care. As one hospital in the northeast of England reported:

The maternity unit has had to buy a new operating table that can hold up to 40 stone (254 kg) in weight. It is regularly in use, as around half of obese pregnant women end up having a Caesarean section.[7]

This may sound like an extreme case, but it is becoming commonplace around the UK hospital network. Obesity does tend to have unexpected consequences, and these do have a noticeable impact on wider society – as the 'regular' use of this operating table would imply. The factors contributing to the growing epidemic therefore deserve to be scrutinized very carefully, and the motives of the food industry clearly fall squarely into this category.

Food manufacturers may not have caused the obesity epidemic, but they have become well versed in exploiting it to their considerable advantage. The more we eat, the more of their products they sell, and, of course, the more they sell, the greater their profits will be. In a consumer-oriented society, food is one of the prime candidates for conspicuous consumption, and it is all too easy for anyone to fall prey to this. Food is, after all, a necessity in our lives, and the desire for it arises at regular intervals every day. As far as the food industry is concerned, the shorter these intervals become the better, and manufacturers and retailers have a vested interest in increasing the frequency of our cravings – by, for example, encouraging us to eat more snacks between meals – as advertising is always urging us to do as a boost to our energy levels. The food industry is selling something we want, and take pleasure from, so we are receptive to its presentation of its products, and the claims made for them.

It is not just a case of responding to greed either; food manu-facturers can help to increase the incidence of obesity by tailoring their products to suit our addictions – the addiction to sugar being prominent among these. Humanity's liking for sweetness is well documented, and foods that satisfy this craving tend to sell extremely well indeed – almost any of us can succumb to the prospect of a sugar rush at some time or other. We seem to start off in life with an innate attraction to sweet things, and most children develop a considerable appetite for these at an early stage. Sugar is an analgesic, and in the past hospital staff sometimes used it as a method of pain relief for babies, as it appeared to have a soothing effect on them (although its success in this regard has been disputed by some studies of late). If parents are of the same disposition regarding sweet products, then they are very likely to pass on their dietary preferences to their offspring. Overweight families are a common enough sight – the 'sweet tooth' takes root easily in this context. From this start, where sugar plays such a positive role, it is hardly surprising that the appetite for sweet things can continue well into adult life. Chocolate manufacturers have long since recognized this, and are constantly engaged in developing new lines of products to appeal to the public's sweet tooth. Confectionery is a very profitable market.

To increase the sweetness quotient of almost any product, whether it is savoury or naturally sweet, is to increase its attractiveness to the general public – a fact of which the fast food industry is very well aware. Combining sugar and salt is almost always a winning move, hence the popularity of recipes involving salted caramel and chocolate, variations on which can be found on the dessert menus in restaurants throughout the UK these days. It is a dish guaranteed to push up an individual's calorie intake, and thus their weight; sugar plus salt has that effect when consumed on a regular basis, and it can quickly become an addictive habit. I noticed a small salted caramel tartlet on sale in a local coffee shop the other day, listing its calorie count on the price tag as 612 – all that for a small snack, little more than a couple of mouthfuls really, to accompany your coffee. There is no way that snacks of this kind could ever be a recommended part of your daily intake, not if you are being at all careful about your weight. My home country of Scotland has the stigma of deep-fried Mars bars to live with in this respect, and deep-fried shortbread is a further addition to Scotland's catalogue of culinary sins. (Scots also have a reputation for miserliness, but I will let that one pass.)

Sugar is now regarded by the medical profession as posing a very considerable risk to public health, even more so than salt, and we are recommended to reduce our intake of it wherever we can. It has been estimated that as much as 80 per cent of the food products on sale in supermarkets these days contain added sugar, so we have our work cut out for us in changing our eating habits: circumstances are not always on our side.[8] Both sugar and salt are necessary elements in our diet, but the amount of each consumed does have to be watched closely. At present, however, we do not seem to be watching anything like closely enough, and our BMI is suffering as a consequence.

As deep-fried Mars bars signal only too well, however, the food industry – both on the manufacturing and retailing side – has other ideas than aiding weight-watching regimes, and it can be very ingenious in putting these into practice. Combining sweet and savoury together tends to hook a substantial proportion of consumers, so the industry has learned to adapt agricultural products to the public preference for sweet over sour, and sweet over bitter, to increase our sugar intake in subtle ways that we might find harder to resist (or worse, even to recognize). Many vegetables on sale in supermarkets are now genetically engineered to lower their sour or bitter taste in favour of an enhanced sweetness, thus indulging an all-too-human weakness. The same effect can be achieved through processing by means of 'debittering', although this carries the risk, as a *New Scientist* article by Marta Zaraska has neatly put it, of 'turning bitter fruit and veg into the junk foods of the fresh produce aisle'.[9] Given the popularity of junk foods and their very prominent role in the obesity epidemic, this can only be regarded as a deeply worrying trend that deserves to be monitored closely.

Debittering produce is bad for our health because of the beneficial effect on our bodies of the compounds and chemicals that bitter-tasting foods contain, as Jennifer McLagan's book *Bitter* points out. She gives the following instructive example:

> What gives grapefruit its characteristic bitter flavor is the chemical naringin, of which there is a higher percentage in white grapefruit than in pink or red. More than half of the world's grapefruit is turned into juice, and during its production the naringin is filtered out in a process called debittering. Not only does this make grapefruit juice less complex in flavor, but it also removes a powerful antioxidant.[10]

Since antioxidants work to neutralize the free radicals in our system, cutting their effectiveness is plainly not a good idea. McLagan recommends squeezing your own grapefruit to obtain the maximum benefit from its juice – sound advice under the circumstances, one would think. Yet as Zaraska notes, white grapefruit is becoming harder to find in greengrocers or on supermarket shelves, because both growers and sellers have discovered that the sweeter pink and red varieties are far more popular with the buying public. Supply is geared towards meeting demand, so pink and red are now dominating the market; an illustration of how volume of sales can have a profound effect on your diet. Sweetness has won out yet again, as unfortunately it usually will.

The debittering process has also been carried out on vegetables, such as broccoli, which is now bred to be far less bitter in taste than in the past – again, to the detriment of much of its nutritional value. Broccoli, in common with the rest of the brassica family, contains glucosinolates, which some studies have claimed helps the body to fight cancer cells. Although this has not been conclusively confirmed, there is general agreement that broccoli and other brassicas are rich in various nutrients that are important to our health, so any process that reduces these is not going to be to our advantage.[11] (It is also interesting to note in this context, that cookery writers are still recommending that we should salt aubergines before using them in their recipes, in order to draw out their bitterness. Bitterness does tend to be looked on as a fault, and its reduction as highly desirable.) Tomatoes, too, which have a certain natural sweetness anyway when they are ripe, can have this quality enhanced by means of genetic engineering. Many consumers appear to find them more palatable once their acidity has been reduced; those that don't will be out of luck, as old-fashioned, 'natural' tomatoes become a hard-to-find speciality item. Supply will, of course, go on meeting demand as long as sales warrant it: not so much the bitter truth as the debitter in this instance. When it comes to food, what the public wants, the public will invariably get – on a plate, in this instance. McLagan tries her best to buck this trend by offering a selection of recipes aimed at making the most of bitter foods, but the issue will increasingly become whether it is possible to get hold of the produce in its natural state in the first place. If supermarkets stop selling bitter fruits and vegetables altogether, there will be an inevitable knock-on effect on the national diet.

Providing the public with what it wants – or feeding its weakness, as it could also be described – is precisely what the fast food industry is set up to do, and it must accept a significant share of the blame for the spread of the obesity epidemic. This is especially the case in countries like the u.s., where fast food has long since become a staple part of the nation's diet, consumed there on a much larger scale than in Europe, to the extent that one commentator has referred to 'the insatiable American appetite'.[12] Fast food has a notoriously high sugar content – children, predictably enough, love it and are only too willing to welcome it as a regular part of their diet. kfc and McDonald's, as obvious examples, are now an integral part of American life, and their presence in Europe and the rest of the world is growing rapidly year by year. The latter company has become somewhat notorious for its policy of aggressively promoting 'super-sized' portions of its meals at a slightly higher price than its standard portions. This is a practice that can only accelerate weight gain in its customers, who are simply increasing their intake of high-calorie food. The filmmaker Morgan Spurlock made a documentary called *Super Size Me* (2004) to show how following the company's promptings to opt for extra-large portions could be harmful to one's health. As an experiment, he ate nothing but McDonald's food for one month, accepting super-size portions when these were offered by staff, to discover what effect this diet would have on his health. This is not a very scientific approach perhaps, with Spurlock being the only test subject (meaning that no general conclusions can be drawn from the experiment); but the subsequent medical checks from his doctor did seem to yield some worrying results even so: his weight increased by 13 per cent, his cholesterol level went up considerably, and he began to build up fat in his liver. One would expect this after the steady consumption of fried chicken, hamburgers and French fries in huge portions, which is all but guaranteed to have an adverse effect on your body's systems.

It is a diet such as the one Spurlock was testing – one high in fats, sugars and salt – that is also implicated in the increasing incidence of Type 2 diabetes in the West. The President of the International Diabetes Federation, David Cavan, has sounded a stark warning about where this trend could lead: 'We're talking about an epidemic that risks not just health systems, which could buckle under the strain, but even entire economies.'[13] This new 'epidemic' is particularly prevalent in cities, where the busy lifestyle, rushed and often hectic, encourages the consumption of fast food. Cities are of course well stocked with fast food vendors, with whole streets full of them being a common sight in most city centres, and rail and bus stations offering prime locations for fast food outlets to supply those of us 'on the run'.

Some European countries, France and Italy in particular, have tried to put up a degree of principled resistance to the overt colonization of their restaurant scene by the American fast food giants, in an attempt to preserve their own highly valued culinary traditions. Italy is even the source of a 'slow food' movement that specifically ranges itself against the encroachment of these giants. As the name suggests, slow food takes a completely different view of how we should consume, emphasizing the social and aesthetic aspects of eating rather than the addictive ones that the fast food industry thrives upon. (An allied ethos that is drawing in adherents in Italy and elsewhere is that of the 'slow city' movement, which is aimed at reducing the pace of city life with its apparently endless streams of traffic and all its accompanying noise and pollution. Several cities and towns – such as Positano and Orvieto (in England, Ludlow has also followed suit) – have put this into practice. An entire lifestyle ethic is contained in that 'slow' tag.) The promise of instant gratification that a McDonald's or KFC meal offers is anathema to slow food enthusiasts, who are utterly opposed to the worldview that lies behind this and campaign vigorously for an attitude that is more firmly rooted in Italian tradition, where food is treated with greater respect and a sense of ceremony. There is a definite cultural divide evident between Old and New World on this subject.

Yet how 'slow food' will fare against junk food in the longer term is more problematical to forecast. Fast food outlets can be found all over Italy now just as easily as in any other Western country, and they have proved to be particularly successful at hooking the younger generation wherever they appear, fitting in with that generation's enthusiastic embrace of an increasing Americanization of their everyday life (influencing, for example, the music they listen to, films they watch and clothing they wear). Traditionalists in both France and Italy are quite rightly concerned about the future of their national cuisine under the circumstances, fearing that the current younger generation may well stick with the fast food/junk food diet that they have taken to so readily.

The junk food industry also holds the advantage of being able to rely on large-scale advertising campaigns to put its message across, and these are, to put it mildly, difficult to avoid in our daily existence. It is an industry that is only too skilled in the dark art of psychological manipulation, with much of this advertising made to appeal very directly to children, who are only too capable of pestering their parents to buy them a fast food meal until they give in to the insistent pressure. Television, the Internet and billboards throughout urban centres (and around major sports stadia too, giving them much wider exposure at televised events) are saturated with images of fast food, planting the message firmly in the public's mind. Routes from airports to cities appear to be favourite sites, lodging the idea in travellers' minds at a point where there is a fair chance that they could be in the market for a quick meal out. It is highly unlikely that you have not seen an advertisement for the fast food giants in the last day or two – unless you steer clear of urban centres altogether, do not read newspapers or magazines and have foresworn the use of most modern technology. Otherwise, you will be exposed sooner rather than later to the blandishments of a fast food purveyor, selling what one particularly critical commentator has called 'degraded industrialized food' to the masses.[14]

The 'obesity epidemic' does raise the tricky issue of whether we are dealing with addiction rather than greed. In other words, can the obese actually help it? Do their cravings, or their responses to these, actually lie within their control? Gluttony somehow seems to imply a more active state than obesity. Gluttony is something you do; obesity something that happens to you. Many factors have to be taken into account here, genetics, for example, or family history (overweight parents or other relatives can create a context in which overeating is simply accepted as the norm and everyone follows suit as a matter of course). Stories circulate periodically in the press about a search for a 'fat gene', which, it's proposed, would have the effect of determining people's eating patterns, thus excusing them from any personal blame. People who are overweight have been known to cite this notion as evidence for their own condition, even though it is unproven and may well constitute a wild goose chase on the part of researchers. A recent study published in the journal *Health Education and Behavior* reported that people who believed in the 'fat gene' tended to eat more than the average, have a less healthy diet overall and exercise less, leading, in something of a self-fulfilling prophecy, to them having a high blood sugar level.[15] Belief in the fat gene seems to be just as bad for you as the fat gene itself – if it existed, that is.

Even if those who are obese really cannot help themselves, however, that does not mean that the food industry should capitalize on the public's addictions in the parasitic way they tend to. Addictions can be encouraged or they can be treated. True, the addiction may not always be cured, or even curable (psychologically this is a very grey area, and there is no clear consensus among the experts), but at least the obesity epidemic will be checked to some degree. The fast food industry has no real interest in checking this, however, no matter what they may say publicly, and despite offering salads on their menus to make them appear more health-conscious. These salads, one suspects, most likely contain debittered vegetables, so are a token gesture at best, particularly if they are served as accompaniments to super-size portions of high-calorie food. Greed creates a market, and our culture is organized in such a way as to supply market demand; this is what markets see as their primary responsibility, especially since it creates higher shareholder returns. While there is clearly an addiction of some kind at play here, we must question whether it is possible to differentiate clearly between addiction and greed. The food industry, however, is hardly helping matters by effectively preying on our weaknesses, indisputably implicating itself in the spread of both the obesity and diabetes epidemics.

There is also profit to be made from obesity in ways other than selling food products. The diet industry thrives on the obesity epidemic, and newspapers and magazines are full of advertisements promoting weight-loss programmes, diet supplements and personal trainers, all designed to help those who are overweight shed their 'unwanted' pounds. The worse the obesity epidemic becomes, the greater the profit margins of the diet industry will be.

It is interesting to reflect on the fact that obesity benefits two such disparate groups, although one could be cynical and say that both depend on the obesity epidemic continuing, as it is particularly fertile ground for the profit motive. There is money to be made from making people overweight, and money to be made in helping them slim down (or attempting to, anyway), so both sides come out winners. Private medical practitioners have also been quick to recognize that there is money to be made in this area, and will provide, for a price, surgical procedures to deal with obesity – the fitting of gastric bands, for example, to reduce the size of the individual's stomach and thus their appetite. In a market-based society, whatever yields profit will be welcomed very warmly.

We might also consider whether we can talk of greed for alcohol, which manifests itself in much the same way as greediness for food; that is, by requiring more and more of an intake so that a person's desire never really seems to be satiated (although I do concede that it is a more problematic condition to pin down in terms of causes).

Heavy drinkers certainly do seem to have a 'hole in their being' that is dictating their actions, and greed is certainly in evidence in supplying what they crave. Medical warnings against the misuse of alcohol are legion nowadays, with guidelines about how many units it is safe for men and women to consume in a week appearing on a regular basis. Doctors will enquire as standard about your alcohol intake if you visit a surgery or go into hospital for any kind of treatment at all, comparing it to the recommended guidelines and commenting if you are above the advised limit. (They will generally recommend that you should decrease your alcohol intake as soon and by as much as possible.) Yet alcohol consumption comes squarely within the issue of the exercise of free will raised earlier. It has to be assumed that individuals make the choice to consume alcohol, in whatever quantity, and interfering with personal choice goes against the grain of the prevailing ideology, with its recognizably libertarian bias. Like fast food, alcohol is advertised very widely in the media, particularly in newspapers, magazines and on billboards, and these are similarly hard to avoid as we go about our daily business. What is critical in both cases is that profits are being made out of human weakness – by the greedocracy.

Official interference may still happen with hard drugs, which are subject to strict regulations and penalties throughout the West. Yet even in that area there are frequent calls by libertarians for a change in the law – as has occurred with soft drugs like cannabis in many instances – on the grounds that it is a denial of consumer choice. This is a society in which consumer choice is taken very seriously: you are supposed to be the one who can decide what to do with your body and your constitution, not the authorities. They can offer advice and guidelines, and can cajole, but they cannot force you to comply with what they say. There may be some restrictions placed on the sale of alcohol throughout the West (these vary from country to country, as does pricing), but it is freely enough available nevertheless, and if you choose to overindulge then there is little to stop you from doing so. In the UK, licensing laws have been loosened considerably in recent years, and bars are allowed to stay open for longer hours than they were for most of the twentieth century. The grounds for this relaxation of the laws is that these longer hours will mean that people are less inclined to drink to excess in a bid to beat the clock at the early closing time that used to apply to UK licensed premises. Yet binge drinking, particularly among the younger generation, has been identified as a concern by many local authorities in recent years.

One of the results of this concern has been a series of campaigns drawing the public's attention to the dangers of overindulgence and binge drinking. One recent such campaign ran under the heading, 'Stay sober for October'; it's a catchy enough slogan, but one wonders just how much impact campaigns like this have on really heavy drinkers, or, more importantly, whether it affects their longer-term habits. What happens when November comes around and then Christmas looms up ahead? Advertising for alcohol products goes into overdrive during the festive period too, which does not make moderation any easier. The UK keeps lowering its recommended intake of alcohol (per day and week) on health grounds, but how effective this is, is open to question too. The new level, introduced in 2016, has become the source of much controversy (and no doubt increasingly awkward exchanges with one's doctor at health checks). If the health authorities are right, then we are heading for the alcohol equivalent of an obesity epidemic – perhaps we are even already there? Opinion does seem to be divided on what constitutes a reasonable intake, however, with the UK's recommended intake being among the lowest in Europe; by way of comparison, Spain sets the recommended limit at two-and-a-half times as high as the UK (as Spain is a major wine producer, this is perhaps not all that surprising). As with food, increased alcohol consumption equals increased profits for an already highly profitable industry; greed, and its consequent lack of moderation, can always be good news to somebody.

Sugar is also present in alcohol products, being part of the fermentation process in brewing and winemaking, so this is yet another source of sugar that many of us probably don't take into account. It is no accident that most younger people gravitate towards the sweeter alcoholic products when they first start drinking – for instance fruit-flavoured ciders, sweetened lager-based drinks and fizzy alcopops. Most wine drinkers eventually shift over to drier (that is, less sweet) wines as they become older, but even these contain some sugar content, which is simply the result of the grapes ripening on the vine. The riper the grapes, the higher their sugar content will be. Warmer-climate wines, with their significantly riper grapes and therefore higher alcohol content, can taste noticeably sweeter than those from more temperate regions (even when classified as dry), unless the latter have been deliberately sweetened to raise the alcohol content.

Neither does global warming help, as the alcohol percentage of most wines has been creeping up steadily for some time now as the climate changes. Where only a few years ago most table wines contained 12–13 per cent alcohol, today this is more likely to be 14–15 per cent; this means a correspondingly greater sugar intake for the wine drinker. The exact role of climate change in this trend is still being debated, and it has been suggested that the consumer has to share at least some of the blame, in that higher alcohol wines tend to be very popular among the wine drinking population. This is yet more proof of sugar's insidious impact, perhaps: push up the sugar content, push up the sales. With no end in sight to global warming – which will certainly make it easier to produce the more alcoholic wines that are meeting with such noticeable consumer approval – we might well wonder how much higher these percentages could rise (table wines at over 16 per cent are not unknown even now). The higher the percentage of alcohol in beer, then the sweeter that will be too. Even brut champagne, about as dry as wine ever gets, still has a sugar content; it is just lower than the norm. (Some champagne houses produce an extra brut, which can be entirely without dosage – that is, sugar added during fermentation. Even those who prefer their wine dry can find this a somewhat challenging drinking experience. It is not all that common, however, and something of a niche product.)

Whether we call it gluttony or not, it is undeniable that excessive consumption of food, particularly of the sweeter kinds of food (and drink, soft as well as alcoholic), is responsible for a multitude of problems in Western society. Health suffers, public finances suffer (as do personal finances, and thus also family life in many cases) and overall quality of life is adversely affected. Profits, however, increase considerably; so there is a vested interest in encouraging this kind of greed, even if it means encouraging the addictive side of our personality, because the sad truth is that addiction equals profit. Greed and profit complement each other very effectively indeed in the neoliberal universe.

6

A BITTER PILL?
HEALTHCARE AND GREED

Healthcare in general is an area in which greed has considerable scope to operate, and this has to be a matter of concern. Health is surely too fundamental a phenomenon to be left to the vagaries of the market, as it is in all too many instances globally, from doctors' and hospital fees to prescriptions. The pharmaceutical industry, 'Big Pharma', is notorious for its pricing policy with regard to newly developed drugs, many of which are proving far too expensive for large sections of the world's population to purchase. The private healthcare system that is the norm in most countries regards health as a source of profit, and can be very difficult indeed for the poor to access properly. We only have to consider the current situation in the U.S. to see an instructive example of this in action, with a substantial number of the country's citizens unable to afford the healthcare insurance required to cover medical treatment. Private medicine has also spotted the potential offered by practices such as cosmetic surgery, and this has developed into a growth industry – for those fortunate enough to be able to pay for its services, that is.

Greed is becoming an antisocial trend throughout the healthcare industry, and this has important implications for all of us – healthcare being a universal need, not some luxury purchase. Life does not become a misery because you cannot afford an expensive new car or technological gadget, but it does if you cannot afford a crucial operation. Many in the UK consider the country's public health service, the NHS, to be one of the greatest achievements of British society in modern times, but it has been the subject of repeated government intervention in recent years that has aimed to gradually privatize it. To counter the policy, a 'Keep Our NHS Public' campaign has been established. The campaign's website describes its attitude towards creeping privatization as follows:

> Keep Our NHS Public's aim is to stop this by opposing cuts and attempts to 'market' NHS services. We aim to create a movement that will mean politicians reinstate our comprehensive, fully funded, publicly run and publicly accountable NHS. Not the empty brand for private profit it's slowly decaying into.[1]

Yet the creeping privatization programme continues apace all the same, with the private sector being brought in to run an increasing number of the service's internal operations. The upshot is that various companies are now making a profit out of healthcare in a system that was set up to be the antithesis of for-profit medical care – a model from which the rest of the world could learn. The pharmaceutical industry, of course, has been making substantial profits out of the NHS since the system was established in the 1940s.

Big Pharma is at the forefront of developing new drugs for some of the world's most deadly diseases: cancer, AIDS/HIV and the recent outbreaks of Ebola virus in Africa are cases in point. Research into finding cures for all of these is ongoing, as it should be for humanitarian reasons, and research of course costs money. The major pharmaceutical firms do spend a lot on research and development, and naturally enough they expect a return for what in some instances can take years of work and investment before a product ever reaches the market. It is when it comes to the price charged for such new drugs that the problems arise. These can put a massive strain on the budgets of publicly funded healthcare systems, and raise the cost of medicines for patients in the private sector by a very noticeable amount. In the U.S. this has even prompted many to start buying drugs outside the country in places where they are significantly cheaper, such as Mexico and Canada. Cross-border tours are even organized for senior citizens, with the express purpose of giving them an opportunity to stock up on cheaper medication, which is either a triumph or an indictment of entrepreneurial capitalism, depending on how you choose to look at it. One company offering these trips, based in Scottsdale, Arizona, has referred to the tours as 'drug runs', which lays its purpose on the line in no uncertain terms.[2] A favoured destination is the Mexican border town of Los Algodones, which is now full of pharmacies, as well as dentists' and doctors' surgeries, to cope with incoming tours. As a recent report on the phenomenon of 'medical tourism', puts it: 'It happens in two different worlds, much to the disapproval of the Food and Drug Administration and the approval of citizens' wallets.'[3]

It is in the developing world, however, that the biggest problems come to light concerning prescriptions. Many of the population there simply cannot afford the price that Big Pharma is asking for many drugs, particularly newly developed ones for conditions such as AIDS and HIV – and cross-border drug runs are not an option available to them. The fact that the countries worst affected by AIDS are in the developing world only compounds the problem, because in particularly poor countries such as these the healthcare system is fairly rudimentary. AIDS has ravaged the population in many parts of Africa. Around 6 per cent of the population of Kenya is HIV positive and therefore at risk of developings AIDS, especially if not treated, while South Africa's rate, currently the highest in the world, is around the 10 per cent mark (in both cases, the percentage is much higher if only the adult population is taken into account). It has become something of an international scandal that many are dying throughout Sub-Saharan Africa, or at the very least suffering needlessly, because of an inability to afford the appropriate treatment for a range of medical problems like this. Even if there is at the moment no totally reliable cure for AIDS, the condition can be managed by antiretroviral drugs and life at least prolonged, often by several years. For this to be beyond the means of many has to be considered a social injustice, even if the situation is improving and the rates are beginning to fall. Even so, the contraception, or contraceptive advice (around the use of condoms, for instance), that could reduce the incidence of AIDS at much lower cost, is still beyond what the bulk of the population can realistically afford in such poor economies. (Religious and cultural barriers also exist to the use of contraception, of course.)

While allowing for the fact that, given the way Western economies are constructed at present, there has to be a return on time and resource invested in research (the public sector is not being granted the necessary funding, after all, meaning it cannot really compete), the size of that return is a critical issue. Every time an outbreak on the scale of the AIDS epidemic occurs, Big Pharma's policies become a topic of heated public debate. Yet even when short-term solutions are cobbled together (perhaps through UN intervention, or charities fundraising for the purchase of the necessary drugs for afflicted countries), on the open market there is nothing to prevent companies from setting whatever prices they choose. 'Whatever the market will bear' is the principle they operate by, as essentially the whole private sector does. It is ultimately greed that lies behind such pricing, because there is no question that the international pharmaceutical giants rake in huge profits for years after the successful development of new or improved drugs. This means that their shareholders are entirely happy with the company's policies, but not those outside of this charmed circle, especially the poor in the developing world who are unable to pay the going rate for their products. Given that what we are talking about is a life-or-death matter in many instances, as it most definitely can be with AIDS, this is hardly a satisfactory situation, and it does invite pointed questions about the ethics of the free market system. It is hard to think of health as just another commodity for sale; few of us feel like consumers when we are going into hospital for a serious operation, for example.

Private medicine certainly seems to create a conflict of interest in its practitioners in a country like the UK, since most of the doctors practising in this sector will have been trained by, and worked in, the NHS. In effect, the UK taxpayer is helping to fund the private system by supplying it with highly qualified personnel; the private system offers no such training programme, making it parasitic on the public. The lure of the private sector is that either it provides an extra source of income for those only working there on a part-time basis and continuing to work in the NHS concurrently, or it opens the way to a much larger regular salary for those who embrace private practice full-time. In the main, however, private hospitals are staffed by NHS consultants working on a part-time basis, and one of their selling points is that they can provide a speedier service than usually offered by the public service. If you are unhappy about being put on a long waiting list for an elective operation within the NHS (some specialisms are more under strain than others in this respect, as are some hospitals), then you can always decide to go private, and you might well make enquiries of the public consultant you are already seeing about your condition. That particular consultant may not work in the private system (those who don't tend to take a principled stand on this, laudably enough), but if they do then they will probably direct you towards the appropriate channels to make the required arrangements. In this way NHS waiting lists can work to the benefit of the private system, and of course the consultants who work there.

Although private practice can be found throughout the UK, the bulk of it is in London; Harley Street, in particular, has become indelibly linked with private medicine in the public consciousness. London offers a particularly well-heeled clientele who are fully prepared to pay the going rate for preferential treatment, meaning that private practice in the capital can be financially very rewarding, putting practitioners in a very different earnings bracket from those on an NHS salary alone. One could be critical, but in a society as firmly based on laissez-faire principles as ours, commercialism will colonize every area it can.

Cosmetic surgery has become big business in the U.S. and is increasingly popular in the UK and Europe, and it certainly appeals to a well-heeled clientele able to indulge their own whims and fancies. There are cases where cosmetic surgery is a genuine health issue, involving the physical well-being of the patient (breast reduction to ease back pain, for example), and thus a legitimate treatment for a public health system to provide. In the majority of instances, however, it has far more to do with personal vanity, generated by some ideal notion of beauty that the customer wants to live up to. The procedures include face lifts, breast enlargement (or reduction where it is purely on the basis of improving one's appearance) and various treatments involving Botox. Whether servicing personal vanity is a valid activity for the medical profession to be engaged in has to be highly questionable. There is a market for it, however, in a society that lays as much emphasis on appearance as ours so obviously does (to the point of overvaluing it, it could easily be argued), and whenever a market emerges, providers will soon follow to exploit its opportunities for profit.

Not all cosmetic surgery is carried out by medically qualified personnel, although it is still on the fringes of the healthcare industry even so. Some Botox treatments can be administered by non-medics in the private sector, but within the NHS these are only available if the injection involves pain reduction, or relieves some chronic condition, such as muscle spasms or spasticity after a stroke. Most of the time, however, treatments of this kind are entirely to do with personal vanity, and they do come with a certain risk factor attached. They can have a different effect from the one promised and that the customer is expecting, perhaps even altering one's appearance for the worse. The result can be very obvious to others, much to the chagrin of the Botox recipient, who will be stuck with the adverse effect for a variable length of time. The only reason for providing such a service is to cash in on human vanity, and as well as carrying some risks it is also expensive.

Private medicine has also become very active of late in the area of human fertility and the provision of IVF treatment. Clinics offer a range of services such as freezing eggs for future use when women decide to delay pregnancy, perhaps when they want to pursue their career for a while longer or have not yet found a partner willing to embark on parenthood. Health conditions such as cancer can also delay or prevent pregnancy, as chemotherapy can destroy fertility. Using private fertility clinics can be a very expensive business, however, and even more questionable is that some clinics' claims about their success rates have been disputed by the UK's Human Fertilization and Embryology Authority (HFEA). The clinics, however, can run up substantial profits for treatments, so greed is winning out over any scruples they may have. Perhaps their ethics leave something to be desired? The current cost of egg harvesting in London is several thousand pounds for a cycle, and it can take several cycles to achieve a pregnancy (not that this can be guaranteed), plus extra charges for storage and other tests and checks before and after the procedure. Quite obviously this will only be accessible to a certain percentage of the population, just as cosmetic surgery is – although the latter has to be considered a far less defensible practice.

One of the pioneers of IVF treatment, Lord Robert Winston, has been very critical of the system overall, which he worries may be exploiting women and in many cases building up their hopes unrealistically, suggesting there could well be an ethical issue at stake. For one thing, success rates drop sharply with age, reducing to only around 3–4 per cent for women in their mid-forties.[4] Winston is particularly sceptical about the wisdom of continuing with treatment for this age group. The primary consideration of fertility clinics, however, is to exploit a market, and as one report notes, 'Britain's fertility industry is booming' at present.[5] There is a demand, so suppliers will keep offering the service; capitalism is never slow to recognize where there is money to be made.

The healthcare insurance industry in the United States is a very lucrative business indeed, and it regularly turns in very large profit margins. So expensive are the policies on offer that a significant proportion of the u.s. population (estimated at around 10 per cent, even after the recent introduction of state-supported Obamacare) has decided it cannot afford the premiums involved, and is simply going without insurance altogether. Given that everyone experiences illness or poor health at some point in their lives, this is a notably risky strategy to adopt, and no doubt the cause of much anxiety at family level. Luck alone will not protect you; health is in many respects a lottery, and no one can ever be sure how they will fare, regardless of how healthy their lifestyle is. Debate rages over this state of affairs in the u.s., which is after all one of the richest countries in the world and certainly the leading economy, and Obamacare (which the private insurance industry fairly predictably opposed bitterly right to the very end) represents an attempt to redress the current imbalance. For the bulk of the population, however, healthcare policies remain a big drain on their finances.

Neither is healthcare insurance a fail-safe purchase. Most policies demand that at least part of the cost of treatment is met by the holder, and companies usually set limits on what they will pay out for the care of any given condition. Premiums also tend to rise when you are elderly, because that is the group most likely to suffer ill-health and require extensive, and accordingly expensive, treatment – there is little evidence here of a caring society. Health insurance providers are always on the lookout for ways to offset the cost of expensive care, and are as a result becoming very interested in methods of forecasting one's likely future health through genetic testing. This is an area that is receiving a lot of research funding at present, and its findings are being widely disseminated by the media. It has even created a market for personal genetic testing kits (such as those produced by the American company 23andMe), despite the fact that making projections based on the data the tests generate is still a very contentious issue, as has been pointed out by bodies such as the u.s. Food and Drug Administration (FDA).[6] Social commentators also express concern that genetic testing could lead to many health insurance applicants being excluded from purchasing any coverage at all by the companies involved, because they do not look like being sources of profit: 'genetic discrimination', as it has been dubbed. Family history, which does not even require genetic testing, can also lower your chances of being eligible for health insurance, or at the very least drive up the cost of your premiums – sometimes exorbitantly, to the point where you might not feel able to afford them. Reducing the risk to their profit margins is always going to be of as much interest to companies in the health business as it is elsewhere, and they are not going to take what to them may appear to be undue risks.

Most companies also adopt a very robust attitude towards claims assessment, and it is by no means guaranteed that these will always be covered anyway. Companies eagerly search for loopholes to prevent liability, with staff employed for precisely that purpose. Such members of staff are highly valued, and they have every incentive to find reasons to reject claims, as it can lead to bonuses – an example of the 'unacceptable face of capitalism'. No doubt some claims actually are false or frivolous (greed can be a factor on either side of the fence), but the underlying principle at work is not exactly patient-oriented. Viewed from the outside, it can all appear to be a deeply cynical exercise, as if the point of the system is to extort as much money as possible from the client base while offering as little as it can get away with in return. Profit is being privileged over physical well-being, which seems to be completely against the spirit of medicine as a human endeavour. That is not the way the vast majority of doctors view their work, and their professionalism is not at issue here, but when the bills are submitted, this is the culture in which the patients' claims will be scrutinized. Somebody will have to pay, and the insurance company will do its very best to push the responsibility back to the policy holder whenever it thinks it can.

It is, then, very much a case of let the buyer beware, but most of the population has no option but to comply, hoping they can recoup at least some of the cost involved – as well as hoping that they never contract a really serious illness that could break them financially (u.s. hospital fees are notoriously high). When dealing with something as basic as health this is an unhappy situation all round, at the very least creating unnecessary stress and worry among many of the country's citizens. Greed is coming squarely up against social need, as the free market allows it to. Neoliberals argue that applying market principles is the best way to guarantee personalized care and improve efficiency, in healthcare as anywhere else; but these are meaningless notions if you don't have the means to pay in the first place. It must also be distinctly depersonalizing to be forced to think of yourself as a profit resource, there to be mined for others' benefit.

There is also an unofficial healthcare industry that preys upon the general public, peddling remedies and treatments that usually have little, if any, scientific validity to recommend them. At one time it was slightingly referred to as 'quack medicine' (peddled by 'snake oil' salesmen and the like); now, however, it goes under the more respectable heading of 'alternative medicine', or sometimes 'complementary medicine', and it is a thriving area. Many of those involved in the sector believe in it quite sincerely, as do many of their clientele, and some alternative medicines do seem to work, or at least offer some measure of symptomatic relief. Yet it is still in the main a method of making profit out of a gullible public. (It should also be noted in this context, however, that placebos have been known to have an effect of symptomatic relief in many clinical trials, so that outcome alone is no proof of efficacy.) No number of failed scientific trials seems to dampen the demand for such remedies significantly, and sadly this all too often comes from individuals with conditions that standard medicine seems unable to cure. Alternative medicine offers at least the possibility of a miracle cure, and that is enough to keep pulling in customers – especially the desperate.

A cynical viewpoint would suggest that alternative medicine could be classified as taking money from people under false pretences. Its practitioners would deny this vociferously, of course, regarding themselves instead as challenging the medical status quo and its entrenched guardians and authorized methods. The attitude is often that the profession of medicine is too set in its ways and just not open enough to new ideas of the type alternative medicine is vigorously pursuing, or to reviving older, traditionally popular ones, such as alternative medicine is providing; a reference to some long-lost wisdom of the ancients is always capable of exerting some appeal. While some folk remedies have turned out to have scientific validity, by no means all of them have, although all kinds of such products are now readily available from alternative medicine suppliers if you feel like trying your luck with any of them.

Homeopathy is a particularly well developed branch of alternative medicine, and one that does not hesitate to claim scientific credentials, even though these are routinely rubbished by the scientific press. In the UK homeopathy has been given a considerable boost in popularity by the patronage of the royal family, with the Prince of Wales an enthusiastic advocate. This affords homeopathy at least a measure of public protection, which it has not been slow to turn to its advantage. One of the consequences is that despite the scepticism of the medical profession in general, there have been homeopathic hospitals operating within the NHS system, although many have now closed. The Department of Health is currently conducting a review which could lead to a ban on GPs prescribing homeopathic remedies, on the grounds that their lack of proven effectiveness constitutes poor use of taxpayers' money. Homeopathy does stretch the boundaries of scientific credibility quite considerably with its principles. There is the 'similarity principle' ('let like be cured by like'), for example, which states that a substance that would cause illness if taken in a large dose, can effect a cure if administered in a minute quantity. Although there are arguably echoes here of the methods used when vaccination was introduced to counter smallpox back in the eighteenth century, where a minute amount of the virus is administered with the aim of building up an immunity to the disease within the patient's system, in homeopathy 'minute' is carried to quite absurd lengths. The process involves diluting the original dose over and over again to the point where, as far as scientists are concerned, none of its molecules at all are left. For scientists, this renders homeopathy a total waste of time – not to mention money.

The argument of the medical profession tends to be that if and when scientifically verifiable evidence is forthcoming that any procedure or treatment from alternative medicine works, and does so consistently using approved testing methods such as randomized trials, then it will be worth bringing into the official medical repertoire – at which point it will stop being 'alternative'. This can happen on occasion, as it has with acupuncture. Once viewed in the West with a great deal of suspicion, acupuncture is now used in some health services, since there is scientific evidence that it can have the effect of stimulating nerves beneath the skin to release endorphins, which can work to relieve pain. Tests consistently demonstrate, however, that homeopathic remedies score about the same 'success' rate as placebos do, and this has repeatedly been pointed out by the UK's National Institute for Health and Care Excellence in its regularly updated NICE guidelines for the medical profession. As a result the UK government, as well as many others around the globe, has counselled the public against the use of homeopathic treatments. The World Health Organization has also come out against homeopathy, but in the UK at least, royal patronage has been enough to give it a foothold in the NHS despite official disapproval and a complete lack of anything resembling proper scientific evidence for its claims. Should future members of the royal family not share this enthusiasm, however, then one suspects it would probably vanish from the official system fairly rapidly (if the Department of Health does not succeed in removing it in the meantime). At present there is a distinct lack of support for homeopathy from UK medical staff. In the French hospital system, however, homeopathy is far more widely available, so it is not without its supporters within the profession elsewhere.

There is a whole range of products available, including foods, that claim to improve general health and well-being, and these are frequently couched in pseudo-scientific language well calculated to fool the unwary. Almost any of us might be taken in by these, even if only momentarily, but help is at hand. *New Scientist* takes great delight in debunking these on a regular basis on its 'Feedback' page, encouraging its readers to send in any new examples they may come across – which they frequently do. The journal has coined the mocking term 'fruitloopery' to describe the way these claims are presented and their misguided way of drawing on science to promise the most improbable outcomes. Since there is no shortage of such claims being made by the alternative medicine industry, there must be a market for such products, and markets do abhor a vacuum.

Claims can be made for such products that contradict basic chemical laws and promise implausible – to the *New Scientist*, more like impossible – physiological effects. *New Scientist* invites us to consider the following from Source Energy Medicine:

> a 'very special' piece of card, with instructions to tape it to the outside of a clear bottle of water. The water would then read the number on the card and dutifully rearrange its structure to become charged with special healing properties.[7]

As *New Scientist* puts it, tongue firmly in cheek, this is 'just the thing for card-carrying members of the alternative-medicine scene' (an appropriate Christmas or birthday present for one of them perhaps?).[8] What's more, the company even produces cards tailored to various types of animals, such as your cat or dog, which no doubt increases their potential market among alternative medicine's pet-loving clientele. The same issue of the magazine also reports a reader finding various products offering back braces making use of magnets 'to boost circulation and so forth', including one where the magnets 'strive to retune disrupted magnetic impulses' causing back pain.[9] Fruitloopery strikes again! Although someone must be buying such things or they would not continue to be produced.

New Scientist suggests that if the word 'quantum' crops up on the product's label, or in its advertising, that alone should be enough to alert the average *New Scientist* reader to the distinct possibility that pseudoscience might be about to put in an appearance. Just try disputing a claim with an apparently quantum explanation if you are not a scientist. Quantum physics is, to put it mildly, a mysterious area of modern science, baffling even to most practising scientists. As the physicist Richard Feynman once provocatively declared: 'I think I can safely say that nobody understands quantum mechanics.'[10] The implication is that it is just too weird to be completely understood by anyone, scientist or not, since it contradicts the general principles behind what has come to be called the 'standard model' in physics, as well as basic logic. Schrödinger's cat, which is simultaneously dead and alive, is only one of the many counter-intuitive consequences that quantum physics asks us to accept. To the general public this air of mysteriousness lends quantum physics an almost magical quality, so any claim to be harnessing the power of its effects tends to be regarded as a signal that some deep process must be going on, counterintuitive or not. Few know enough about quantum physics to question what is being said anyway. *New Scientist* journalists and readers, however, do know enough (even if, as Feynman insists, this can never amount to total understanding of the quantum world), and they are only too willing to pour scorn on the products' makers for trying to mislead the consumer. ('Quantum' has even made its way into marketing research terminology, with one consultancy, Qual360, offering its clients 'ground-breaking advances in understanding complex consumer behaviour through quantum physics'.[11])

Given that few of us have science degrees, claims of this nature are trading on the general consumer's ignorance – even if it hardly seems credible that anyone could be taken in by something quite as far-fetched as labels radiating healing power into water molecules, which sounds more like alchemy than science. Were this to be described in a work of science fiction, we could probably suspend our disbelief long enough to accept it, but in real-life medicine? The claims really do leave a bitter taste in the mouth, since they cast the manufacturers' motives in a very unflattering light. If anyone at all in the company's management structure does have scientific training (or even a modicum of it), then they must know that the effects being claimed for their product cannot be true; that they are flights of fancy at best. This once again recalls the notion of gaining money under false pretences, and it does look very much as if the public's gullibility is being preyed upon – quite possibly by the unscrupulous. If this point of view constitutes cynicism, then I am more than happy to own up to it.

7

FROM COLONIALISM TO NEOCOLONIALISM: THE POLITICS AND GEOPOLITICS OF GREED

Nations are every bit as capable of being self-centred and greedy as individuals are, and we need look no further than the history of colonialism for proof of this contention. Colonization is a well-established fact of human existence, and there have been constant movements of peoples from territory to territory in order to gain control of more resources, agricultural and mineral, throughout recorded history. Europe alone yields a host of examples of this phenomenon in premodern times, with migrations from area to area on a regular basis before the concept of national borders, or national sovereignty as we understand it nowadays, came to be established and respected. Even then, there are examples to be cited, such as the Norman invasion of England in 1066. (The Normans were particularly active in this regard, travelling from their original Scandinavian base to colonize countries throughout Europe, from France and England, down as far as Sicily in the Mediterranean.) In the modern period the activity became institutionalized in the form of colonialism, with the major European powers of the nineteenth and early twentieth century competing vigorously with each other to take control of the material resources throughout the lesser developed world that their own rapidly industrializing societies, and national ambitions, demanded. The political motivation in almost every instance was to improve the trading position, and thus the wealth, of the nation, and it was plainly successful in that endeavour until well into the twentieth century. Some colonies exist to this day (if merely a shadow of before). 'Possessive individualism' applies to nation states as well, and national self-interest can be just as single-minded as the individual variety, even to the point of going to war to achieve its objectives. Colonialism breeds violence, both against rivals and subject populations.

In the contemporary world, the rise of neoliberalism and globalization has led to a neocolonial situation, with the West exploiting the developing world for the cheap manufacture of consumer goods to be sold on the Western market, endowing Western powers with considerable influence in these developing countries. The Chinese economy, as a case in point, is heavily based on this process, and the label 'Made in China' is now ubiquitous in Western shopping centres. The effect is to increase the wealth of the corporate sector, particularly the multinationals, to an unprecedented degree, given that their operating costs have fallen dramatically through the policy of outsourcing their production. This explains the economic plight of once thriving manufacturing centres like Detroit, which was stripped of its very reason for existence after the loss of most of its automobile manufacturing industry in the later twentieth century, and saw its population dwindle in consequence. All Western countries can point to their own examples of such rapid decline in the last few decades.

It is also interesting to note in this context that China has of late been trying its hand at a neocolonialist-style policy in Africa, in a bid to corner the supply of trade and resources in underdeveloped countries in the way that the West pioneered. The Chinese have learned only too well from the West in that respect, and the geopolitical commentator Tim Marshall has reported just how extensive their interests are becoming throughout the continent: 'The Chinese are . . . building ports in Kenya, railway lines in Angola, and a hydroelectric dam in Ethiopia. They are scouring the length and breadth of the whole of Africa for minerals and precious metals.'[1] As far as Africa is concerned, the next generation of neocolonialism would appear to be well and truly under way.

Both neoliberalism and globalization encourage greed on an unhealthy scale, to the point where many commentators are expressing fears that it is distorting the social balance in the West no less than in the developing world. There is now, as Guy Standing has theorized, a 'precariat' class in the West, which endures a difficult existence of part-time (often seasonal) employment, cut off from the fringe benefits that previous generations of workers in the West had come to take for granted, benefits such as holiday pay, pension schemes and sick pay. The precariat may well be switching between various kinds of activity, as Marx suggested would become the norm in a communist utopia, where we would follow up different tasks and occupations as we chose, and as our interests led us, but they are doing so minus the economic security that Marx's vision assumed would be in place. For the precariat such adaptability is a necessity rather than an aesthetic choice, and it is not anything like the idyll portrayed by Marx in *The German Ideology*; instead, it is a state of insecurity and worry about the ability to meet basic living costs.

Commentators are beginning to predict that precarianism may well represent the future of work, and that full-time, permanent employment will soon be a thing of the past. Wealth at the lower end of the socioeconomic scale is systematically falling, while at the upper end it is rising significantly, and the phenomena are intimately connected: the greediest are currently very much in the ascendancy, and the precariat are having to scrabble for whatever they can get. This is the big dilemma that neoliberalism has bequeathed to the world, and governments collectively seem desperately short of solutions to it at present (or effective ones at any rate). Paul Mason's book title *Meltdown: The End of the Age of Greed* notwithstanding, future historians may well look back on this period as the 'Age of Greed'.

Modern colonialism was based on greed for both land and resources, and national self-interest was pursued ruthlessly by the European colonial powers. They recognized no rights of the indigenous population of the territories that were taken over, often by brute force and with many casualties. Huge swathes of the globe were simply appropriated by the leading European nations, and turned into outposts of empire. The continent of Africa, for example, was systematically parcelled up bit by bit over the course of the nineteenth century without regard for local sensibilities, as Marshall points out:

> Back in the great capital cities of London, Paris, Brussels and Lisbon, the Europeans then took maps of the contours of Africa's geography and drew lines on them – or, to take a more aggressive approach, lies. In between these lines they wrote words such as Middle Congo or Upper Volta and called them countries . . . Many Africans are now partially the prisoners of the political geography the Europeans made.[2]

The greed for more territory seemed insatiable. One has only to consider the size of the empire that Britain contrived to assemble by the late nineteenth century to discover just how insatiable (this empire still exists today in the somewhat ghostly form of the Commonwealth). The British Empire was truly enormous, spanning the globe and pouring wealth back into the mother country, further inflating the fortunes, and fuelling the greed, of those at the top end of the socioeconomic scale. That may not have been the only rationale that lay behind it – there were complex geopolitical motives at work too – but it was how it worked out in practice, serving as a conduit for greed. A similar system was operating in the other main European nations, with France, Germany, Belgium and the Netherlands all benefitting significantly from the output of their own colonies, as did Spain and Portugal (even earlier into the colonial game). Britain, however, was clearly the most successful empire in terms of its overseas holdings, and the wealth these brought was a key factor in Britain becoming one of the world's major political powers.

Rivalry between the major colonial empires was the source of much tension, and contributed significantly to the build-up to the First World War. Germany in particular was desperate to build up an overseas empire, as it was a late-comer to the colonization process, having only become a unified nation in 1871. Germany was only too aware of what colonies could be worth, observing the wealth that colonialism was delivering to rivals like France and Britain, and it wanted its share of the enterprise in order to compete more effectively with them on the world stage: greed and geopolitical ambition form a potent combination. Like others at the time, Germany targeted Africa, the last significant area of the globe available for colonization in the late nineteenth century. Clashes and 'incidents' were frequent, as the various European powers strove to increase their empires at the expense of each other. There was a notable flashpoint at Agadir, Morocco, in 1911, for instance, when Germany responded to France's attempt to exert more control over the North African country by dispatching a gunboat to the Moroccan port. Germany's conditions for ceasing to pursue its own ambitions in the area included the demand that France cede territory to it in the Congo. Britain soon stepped in to the affair, with soon-to-be Prime Minister Lloyd George strongly warning against such demands in his Mansion House speech of 1911, indicating that he regarded these as a threat to the concept of national sovereignty:

> If a situation were to be forced upon us in which peace could only be preserved by the surrender of the great and beneficent position Britain has won by centuries of heroism and achievement, by allowing Britain to be treated where her interests were vitally affected as if she were of no account in the cabinet of nations, then I say emphatically that peace at that price would be a humiliation intolerable for a great country like ours to endure.[3]

The language Lloyd George used is very revealing. Here colonies are reduced to the status of mere 'interests' of a greater power, without their own identity, and treated as the prize for the greater power's historical 'heroism and achievement'. In real terms it was the colonies that were being treated as if they were 'of no account in the cabinet of nations'. Moreover, 'interests' (like Morocco and the Congo) had to accept that their primary role was to add to the wealth of their colonizers, and that they would go on doing so until they managed to throw off the yoke of their colonial servitude.

The story of European colonization in Africa and Asia is anything but an admirable one, and it required some horrific violence and many outrages to keep the colonized populations suppressed and biddable – even if only grudgingly. This was all in the name of guaranteeing a steady supply of goods and materials back to the colonizing country, thus enriching the members of the ruling class, and particularly its investors, to a phenomenal degree. A large proportion of the national wealth of the colonial powers derived from their colonies, and the system of foreign aid that has developed since the end of the colonial era has hardly constituted adequate recompense for that history. As Piketty has noted: 'In Africa, the outflow of capital has always exceeded the inflow of foreign aid by a wide margin.'[4] Joseph Conrad offers a stinging critique of the colonial system as practised in Africa in places like the Belgian Congo, in his 1902 novel *Heart of Darkness*. As the narrator of the story, Charles Marlow, an employee of a colonial trading company in the region, bluntly puts it: 'The conquest of the earth, which mostly means the taking it away from those who have a different complexion or slightly fatter noses than ourselves, is not a pretty thing when you look into it too much.'[5] Marlow has had ample opportunity to look into it in his role for the company, and although he goes on to offer a defence of the policy, he does not sound completely convinced by it himself:

> What redeems it is the idea only. An idea at the back of
> it; not a sentimental pretence but an idea; and an unselfish
> belief in the idea – something you can set up, and bow
> down before, and offer a sacrifice to . . .[6]

The 'sacrifice' tended to be on the part of the colonized peoples, however, and the manner in which Marlow's defence peters out suggests an unspoken awareness of this uncomfortable fact.

The idea that Marlow is referring to is one that was claimed by all the colonial powers in justification for their expansionist policies: that they were bringing 'civilization' and 'progress' to the territory they had seized, by introducing Western values and technology with all the sociopolitical benefits that were supposed to follow on from being modernized. The history of the Belgian Congo, however, does not inspire much confidence in that idea. The former Belgian colony was stripped of huge quantities of its raw materials by the occupying colonial power in one of the most brutal examples of European colonization on record (and there is no lack of competition for that dubious distinction). While held as a personal fiefdom by King Leopold II from 1885 to 1908 – enriching him enormously even though he never set foot there – it is estimated that as many as ten million of the local African population died. It was 'a death toll of Holocaust dimensions', as Adam Hochschild has summed it up in his study of the Congo's history and its relations with Europe.[7] Forced labour was widely used for road and railway construction, and brutal punishments, such as cutting off hands and feet, were a common occurrence for failing to meet the quotas set by the Belgian authorities for supplying them with valuable items such as ivory or rubber. Even the other colonial nations, none of whom could have an entirely clean conscience about their own performances on this score, particularly when it came to Africa, professed to be shocked by the conditions in the so-called 'Congo Free State'. 'Free' can hardly have been used more ironically than it was in this instance, and there was an ensuing international outrage over Leopold's policies – his reign of 'rubber terror' as it has come to be known.

From 1908 to 1960 the Congo was a colony of the Belgian nation as a whole, and the wealth from its rubber plantations, gold and diamond mining flowed steadily back to Europe. While lucrative for those engaged in running the trade, it did very little at all for the territory's inhabitants, and the Congo has never really succeeded in building up a viable society since. It remains a desperately poor part of the world to this day, racked by war and violence: 'the most under-reported war zone in the world, despite the fact that six million people have died there during wars which have been fought since the late 1990s', as Marshall reminds us.[8] The legacy of the colonial powers in general has not been very positive, and one of the saddest aspects of the aftermath of the colonial era has been the corruption and disorder that has come in its wake in so many countries. (Belgium hardly helped in this by being implicated in the death of the independent Congo's first head of state, Patrice Lumumba, in 1961, which it has since admitted and apologized for.) With very few exceptions, the ex-colonial nations in Africa, in common with the Congo, have struggled to establish stable political regimes, and all too many of them have ended up under dictatorial, one-party rule, where greed has openly flourished at the top. Dictators can amass huge personal fortunes in what is almost a caricature of the colonial system, with the mass of the population being exploited in much the same manner that they were under European rule. The ex-colonial powers surely have to take some of the blame for this, in that they hardly set a very good example when they were in control, being mainly concerned with extracting as much wealth as they possibly could from their colonies. Most of them left little behind in the way of stabilizing institutions.

The 'idea' Marlow speaks of was always questionable anyway, signalling as it did an assumption of advanced cultural development on the part of the colonizing nation. As Edward Said has pointed out in his influential study of the effects of such attitudes on the Middle East, *Orientalism* (1978), 'the idea of European identity as a superior one in comparison with all the non-European peoples and cultures' (exactly what Lloyd George's speech reveals) was the prevailing notion, and that has died hard.[9] Many of those working in the colonial system genuinely did feel they were working towards the cultural and economic betterment of their country's colonies, and took that responsibility seriously. They could be pained at coming up against colonialism's excesses, and sympathize with the local population's bitter feelings about being made subject to these (as even happened in the Congo, helping to make the atrocious situation there known outside, as Hochschild notes). E. M. Forster portrays some such characters in his novel *A Passage to India*, including the College Principal, Fielding, who runs afoul of his fellow colonials for allowing Indians to attend his classes: 'He did succeed with his pupils, but the gulf between himself and his countrymen ... widened distressingly.... The feeling grew that Mr Fielding was a disruptive force.'[10] Yet the truth is that colonialism was far from altruistic. Its guiding principles were largely about appropriating a territory's resources for one's own economic benefit, and the anti-Western sentiment it left behind in its wake is only too understandable. It would have taken more than a few Fieldings to have made colonialism any less detestable to those at the receiving end. The situation in the Congo did improve after King Leopold's day, but his legacy could hardly fail to live on.

In *Heart of Darkness*, Marlow is more than somewhat shocked when he arrives in the Congo and observes what colonialism involves there, witnessing at first hand the extent of the maltreatment of the local population by colonial officials. The sheer inhumanity of it appalls him, and he remarks on the 'deathlike indifference of unhappy savages' when he stumbles upon the spectacle of forced labour near the river station.[11] Even if the Belgian Congo did have a particularly unsavoury reputation, similar things were happening throughout the colonial system. Britain put down several uprisings in India over the course of its time as occupiers with notable severity, events which have left a blot on its national reputation. Nor have they been forgotten in India to this day: the infamous 'Indian Mutiny' of 1857, for example (which admittedly saw atrocities committed by both sides), is often referred to as the 'First War of Independence' in Indian school textbooks. Both Britain and France also hung on to their colonies until well into the twentieth century, and in many, if not most, cases it took a violent revolution for the colonized nations to win their liberty and make the colonists withdraw. Such a history, with greed as the unmistakable impetus behind it, is not easily forgotten.

The bitterly fought Algerian Revolution against French rule in the 1950s illustrates just how reluctant colonial powers could be to lose control of their overseas possessions, even as the colonial era was coming to an end all around the world (Britain, for example, had withdrawn from India, and was beginning to do the same systematically in Africa). France had turned Algeria into a major wine producer, which locked it into the French economy where wine played a central role (as it did culturally). The French settlers in Algeria did very well out of this trade, which was of course anathema to the country's Muslim population given their religion's strict prohibition against alcohol. Roland Barthes very pointedly drew attention to his nation's lack of sensitivity on this issue:

> The mythology of wine can in fact help us to understand the usual ambiguity of our daily life. For it is true that wine is a good and fine substance, but it is no less true that its production is deeply involved in French capitalism, whether it is that of the private distillers or that of the big settlers in Algeria who impose on the Muslims, on the very land of which they have been dispossessed, a crop of which they have no need, while they lack even bread. There are thus very engaging myths which are however not innocent. And the characteristic of our current alienation is precisely that

wine cannot be an unalloyedly blissful substance, except
if we wrongfully forget that it is also the product of an
expropriation.[12]

Barthes was writing before the Algerian Revolution had triumphed
and driven the French out, and wine production was one of the
prime casualties of the aftermath, with many vineyards being
grubbed up as a hated symbol of French occupation. Prior to
the Revolution, wine had been a major export from the country,
with a substantial international market being developed for it, but
although some production still takes place it is on a very reduced
scale compared to its heyday under the French. This is only what one
would expect with a fundamentalist Islamic government in power.

Britain's treatment of the indigenous inhabitants in its many
colonies also left a great deal to be desired. We can trace this right
back to the earliest of these endeavours in the 'new world' of North
America in the seventeenth century, where the English settlers
considered the native tribes to be uncivilized savages, and thus
accorded them no right at all to the land they were occupying. Even
in our own day, the only land their descendants hold title to is on
the various reservations scattered throughout the country, both in
the U.S. and Canada (and these tend to be economically deprived).
A similar attitude was displayed towards the native population of
Australia when colonies were established there in the eighteenth
century. In neither of these cases was the indigenous population
very large, and the settlers soon outnumbered them as they spread
over the territory in successive waves of immigration, in a relentless
expansion, until they occupied the whole of the land mass of the
modern-day continental United States and Australia. Crucially,
too, the settlers carried with them a technology that gave them
immense power over the locals, who had no response to modern
weaponry. India, however, was a very different proposition, vastly
more populous than Britain (by a factor of twenty or so), and with
a settled, hierarchical society rather than the nomadic, largely

hunter-gatherer system found in North America and Australia. India was a colony to be exploited for its resources rather than as a site of European settlement.

Despite the generally critical attitude to colonialism nowadays, there are still some voices speaking up in favour of the empire. The historian Niall Ferguson for one makes a spirited case for British colonialism, arguing that for all its faults it could still be said to have brought more good than bad:

> For better, for worse – fair and foul the world we know today is in large measure the product of Britain's age of Empire. The question is not whether British imperialism was without a blemish. It was not. The question is whether there could have been a less bloody path to modernity. Perhaps in theory there could have been. But in practice?[13]

That is essentially the question that Marlow is groping to find an answer for in *Heart of Darkness*, although he sounds far less confident in tone than Ferguson does about whether 'fair' exceeds 'foul'. Ferguson defends the notion of 'the mission', robustly although not uncritically, and he does concede that Britain made many regrettable mistakes along the way. Ultimately, however, this turns into an ideological issue, whether or not you believe that the cause of modernity justified co-opting other peoples into it, often against their will; they were, after all, the ones being forced to take the 'bloody path', to make the 'sacrifice' Marlow refers to. Not all of us will follow Ferguson in answering yes to the question, which raises some very awkward moral issues. We might note as well that much the same argument is being used by neoliberals to justify the spread of globalization, and in its wake neo-colonialism: effectively, that it is all for your own good. Whether you are being colonized or neocolonized, the system will be imposed on you whether you agree with it or not; greed will ensure that. Without question, both colonialism and neocolonialism are highly profitable activities to engage in – for the stronger party in the relationship, that is, as even Ferguson acknowledges.

One of the regrettable mistakes Ferguson alludes to was Britain's involvement in the transatlantic slave trade, which saw millions of Africans enslaved and transported to North America and the Caribbean. Eventually Britain took the lead in abolishing the slave trade in the nineteenth century, and that does deserve to be put on the credit side of the ledger, but this was not before the trade had seriously enriched plantation owners and various ports like Liverpool and Bristol, where many of the slave traders were based. One story recounted by Ferguson is particularly thought-provoking in this respect. It concerns an eighteenth-century clergyman called John Newton, who in his early career was a slave trader to the West Indies (although even then a devout believer). Ferguson realizes this calls for some explanation:

> We today are of course repelled by slavery. What we find hard to understand is why someone like Newton was not. But slavery made overwhelming sense as an economic proposition. The profits to be made from cultivating sugar were immense; the Portuguese had already demonstrated in Madeira and Sao Tomé that only African slaves could stand the work; and the Caribbean planters were willing to pay roughly eight or nine times what a slave cost on the West African coast.[14]

In this clash between economics and morality, economics wins hands down, and it is as revealing an example of greed as you could wish to find. I admit that it can be anachronistic to judge the morality of earlier ages by our own, yet a tale like this still has relevance to us now. If the profit margin is large enough, then even ostensibly upright individuals can be susceptible to the pull of their economic sense, which can well turn out to be 'overwhelming'. Slavery may well have been outlawed in the Western world, but social conscience is not always proof against the pull of tax evasion, or the prospect of inflated shareholder dividends offered by the various dubious practices – zero-hours contracts and outsourcing of production, for example – that corporations use to drive down outgoings. Faced with a choice between substantial profits and the promptings of social conscience, the chance to aggrandize oneself or do something for the general good, economic sense has a depressing tendency to carry the day – among our contemporaries no less than our eighteenth-century forebears.

It has long been an article of faith among Marxists that colonialism was primarily an economic affair, with the major European powers plundering the underdeveloped world for all it was worth. Lenin in particular took a very strong line on this, denouncing it as an example of capitalist imperialism at its worst. For him it was also a critical factor in the outbreak of the First World War:

> The war of 1914–18 was imperialistic (that is, an annexationist, predatory, plunderous war) on the part of both sides; it was a war for the division of the world, for the partition and repartition of colonies, 'spheres of influence' of finance capital, etc.[15]

While there is a certain amount of truth in this belief that colonialism was economically motivated (and tales such as that of John Newton do provide it with some substance), Western historians nowadays regard it as having been a much more complex phenomenon than that, partly political and partly economic in nature, with many complicating factors at work in both of these categories. On the political side, colonial expansion was as much about trade as anything else, opening up new markets for home products since Western markets were becoming increasingly tariff-ridden throughout the nineteenth century – Britain being an exception in its commitment to free trade. That does add an economic dimension to the political, of course (as did the slave trade), although the connection is by no means as straightforward as Marxists would have it. The political dimension could also include concerns over national security, for example, through the belief that an empire conferred prestige on the colonizing nation, and that not to give priority to building one left a country at risk from being overtaken in the power stakes by its rivals (as Germany came to believe). As D. K. Fieldhouse has noted, colonialism could be interpreted as a desire by some politicians 'to acquire overseas possessions as part of their diplomatic manoeuvring, as strategic bases, as symbols of status, or merely in order to deny geographical areas seen as important to national security to foreign rivals'.[16] Various influences came to bear on European imperialism, and it was never a homogenous movement.

Ferguson, too, is concerned to look past mere economic explanations. He provides a detailed account of the political background that lay behind the growth of the British Empire, much of which did stem from concerns over national security (as Britain conceived of it). The colonization projects of rivals such as France, Spain and the Netherlands were increasing those nations' wealth and international power to the extent that Britain felt that if it did not respond in kind, and aggressively so, then it could find itself cut off from access to many of its markets. Were that to happen, its trade would be severely diminished and its economy would suffer. And so empire-building turned into a complicated game of geopolitics between the major European powers. To his credit, Ferguson does not shy away from acknowledging the violence and atrocities against indigenous populations that were often involved in the construction of Britain's empire (as was true of all other European empires). Yet the thrust of his argument overall is directed towards the notion that 'Britain made the modern world'. Plausible as the case presented is, it does bring to mind some pointed questions. What *kind* of a world did Britain make? And would it appear as appealing to the empire's many colonized nations as to a British-born empire enthusiast like Ferguson?

One can sense why there would be widespread resistance to the expansion of the empire from those colonized when Ferguson notes that, once British rule was firmly established in India from the late eighteenth century onwards, 'despotism remained the preferred political order' – a not uncommon response in the colonial sphere.[17] (Interestingly enough, however, one can still find Hindus willing to praise the coming of the Raj for bringing about the downfall of the Islamic Mughal Empire. The Parsi community remember the Raj as a time of influence and economic security, as high-ranking members of the bureaucrat class.) The economic inequalities generated by despotism could only exacerbate the situation further, with Ferguson observing that

> the average Indian had not got much richer under British rule. Between 1757 and 1947 British per capita gross domestic product increased in real terms by 347 per cent, Indian by a mere 14 per cent. A substantial share of the profits which accrued as the Indian economy industrialized went to British managing agencies, banks or shareholders.[18]

One does not have to be a Marxist to identify a blatant injustice taking place here, nor to see greed as a primary motivating factor. Empire-building may not be a purely economic phenomenon, but there is clearly a lot of money to be made from it, and it is usually an elite of banks and shareholders who turn out to be the main beneficiaries. Neither does one have to be a Marxist to wonder whether the 'redemption' Marlow sought could ever be provided from a record such as Ferguson's statistics reveal. Ferguson, however, concludes that the positive outweighs the negative when it comes to the British Empire's history of colonialism, although it must be emphasized that this is a verdict delivered from the empire side. The perspective from the other angle is very different. There, the negative usually weighs heaviest on the scales, as Said insists. Hence the various campaigns that have been started over the last few decades for reparations, and very substantial ones too, to be made for having been subjected to the colonial experience (Ferguson alludes to these). These campaigns have largely not been successful, although Britain, among others, has made some gestures in that direction. As Prime Minister, Tony Blair offered a general apology for the suffering caused by the slave trade.

Fieldhouse's concern is to put forward an explanation for imperialism that synthesizes the various considerations involved, from the economic through the political and the ideological. For him,

> the fundamental question to be asked about economic imperialism can be re-formulated in the following terms: under what circumstances, in Europe or on the periphery, were European governments in the period 1830–1914 prepared to use political methods to solve economic problems?[19]

Whether it was economics, politics or ideology that were most influential in the development of imperialism, the critical point for this study is that greed was always at play somewhere in the process: either greed for money, greed for resources or greed for power (most likely a synthesis of all three in Fieldhouse's view). The political and the economic were often closely intertwined, as Fieldhouse indicates in remarking that, in Britain's case,

> the Foreign Office accepted that wars for trading opportunities might constitute a justifiable use of public resources provided they were in the interest of the nation as a whole rather than of particular private groups and that at least some notional diplomatic justification based on abuse of treaty rights or international law could be put forward.[20]

It has to be assumed that 'private groups' nevertheless profited considerably from such a policy, and the way in which it removed obstacles to trade, as it did in the example given by Fieldhouse of the 'China wars' to open up that country to British trading enterprises in the nineteenth century. Since these served to further Britain's commercial interests, they met with Foreign Office approval. Economics may not provide the sole explanation for the rise of the British Empire (or any other European empire), as Fieldhouse emphasizes, but it was never a negligible element in the enterprise: John Newton was by no means an isolated case. Greed played its part in colonialism, and continues to do so in neocolonialism.

8

INTERNATIONAL SPORT AND THE GREED FOR FAME AND SUCCESS

In the world of international sport, greed is a significant factor governing the actions of both its administrators and its participants. Financial gain is the primary motivation for the former group, and the institutional power they wield gives them wide scope to indulge their desires in this direction. For the latter, although financial motivations can play a part, it is more a case of greed for success and sporting glory that is in operation. That is a drive that can border on the pathological, often going to the lengths of willingness to use drugs on a scale that is injurious to the athlete's future health, the lure of fame proving overwhelming. Sport is an important element across all of the world's cultures, a public spectacle that gives pleasure to many through the moments of high drama and passion it yields on a regular basis; but what if these are not honestly arrived at, what if we cannot take them at face value? Ethically speaking, there is a lot at stake here.

A high-profile example of institutional greed in sport can be found in the investigations into world football's governing body, FIFA. These have uncovered a web of bribery and corruption among its officials that has shocked the public by its scale. After all, it is not that long since the International Olympics Committee (IOC) went through a similar scandal concerning the awarding of the Olympic Games, with bribes being made by competing venues to win the right to host the event. One would expect that other international sporting bodies would have taken note of the outcry this caused, ensuring that their own system was free of such corrupt practices, but the bidding process for the World Cup has become particularly notorious. It insists on the host nation providing the infrastructure it specifies (as do the Olympics), usually necessitating the building of new stadia and new transport systems to cope with the influx of spectators from around the globe. These facilities can easily turn into white elephants afterwards, as many nations find out to their dismay – especially if they are in the developing world, where public funds could, and no doubt should, be spent on far more worthwhile social projects. Both Brazil and South Africa have found this out to their cost in recent years. In Brazil the financial strain of hosting the 2014 World Cup and the 2016 Olympic Games in such quick succession has sparked public protests and even riots over what many feel are misplaced priorities on the part of the government.

Despite the problems hosting the World Cup can create for host nations, FIFA offers no help with funding itself, even though it is awash with money from television rights and sponsorship deals which yield billions of pounds in revenue. Such is the international prestige associated with hosting the tournament, however, that it generates a culture of bribery by bidders, the extent of which is slowly becoming apparent as the investigations dig ever deeper. The FIFA set-up certainly provides ample opportunity for such unscrupulous demands to be made.

Few among the existing FIFA hierarchy appear to be untainted by the allegations that are flying around in the media.[1] Many senior FIFA officials have already had corruption charges brought against them while in post in their home national football associations, or have even been convicted of misappropriation of FIFA financial grants for their own personal use, so the problem runs deep in global football culture. FIFA demands to be made tax-exempt in the host nation, and it also receives significant tax breaks in Switzerland, the home of its headquarters. Its officers around the world, meanwhile, are awarded regular large bonuses, making it highly desirable to be associated with the organization, and to close one's eyes to any surrounding corruption. The u.s. Attorney General, heading a full-scale inquiry into FIFA's financial dealings which has already led to several arrests and indictments, has spoken of a 'World Cup of fraud' going on. How long that may have been the case it is hard to say, but doubts about past events are predictably beginning to build up. It can make one despair of human nature to see how personal morality can be so easily overcome by the promise of money in secret deals. The situation is so bad that calls have been made to abolish FIFA as it now stands and replace it with a completely new organization to oversee the running of world football. 'It is past time to abolish FIFA,' as a *New York Times* feature declared in 2014, for example.[2]

Hard on the heels of this affair has come what is potentially an even greater crisis for the world of sport than the unfolding FIFA scandal: the revelation in the run-up to the 2016 Rio Olympics of systematic, apparently government-aided in some instances, doping of competitors in international athletics, coupled with charges of corruption against the top officials in the International Association of Athletics Federations (IAAF). Russia was accused of these practices by an investigation conducted on behalf of the World Anti-Doping Agency (WADA). Several Russian officials have been charged with requesting, and subsequently accepting, money from athletes on a regular basis in order to suppress their suspect blood-testing results. Without this assistance, which in some cases has involved the destruction of the relevant blood samples before testing could even be carried out (as reported in the WADA investigation), the athletes would have run the risk of being banned from their sport for taking prohibited substances to improve their performance, as well as being stripped of any medals they had won in official competitions and their names removed from the records. Yet again, greed is to the fore: greed for money on the part of those running the tournaments, and greed for fame on the part of the athletes, national sports organizations and national governments that were apparently implicated (winning a medal can also lead to lucrative endorsement contracts for athletes, as sporting fame so often does nowadays). The prestige of an Olympic medal appears to have overridden all other considerations, and the public has been left wondering whether it can trust the results in such events in future. Whether the IAAF should be abolished and replaced by a new body has openly been discussed in the media (as with FIFA).

It is a sorry tale all round, and it could take years before the full extent of the corruption is known, especially since such charges are invariably met with a chorus of denials by those accused (usually accompanied by the claim that it is all just a conspiracy dreamed up by the media), as were those corruption allegations against the IOC and FIFA until the build-up of evidence became critical. We already have experience of an orchestrated denial culture over doping in the sport of cycling, where successful individuals kept up the pretence for years of being drug-free, until the conspiracy finally cracked in cases such as Lance Armstrong and his team in 2012. The sport's authorities were subsequently forced into a humiliating rewrite of its history of who had won what titles for quite some time back: all seven of Armstrong's Tour de France titles, for example. Many in the sport now concede that the practice was in fact widespread, and there has to be doubt as to whether it has now been rooted out altogether, or just become ever more sophisticated in its procedures to evade detection. Cycling's major competition, the Tour de France, continues to be the focus of considerable suspicion about doping, and this seems likely to linger on – as does the culture of denial. Denials of corruption are now all but expected by the public, who are fast coming to regard them as tantamount to admissions of guilt. 'Innocent until proven guilty' hardly seems to work in the context of top management in the major sports organizations any more; a sentiment unwittingly reinforced by the comment from one such indignant official that he could not be expected to deny something he had not done.

Professional sport seems saturated with examples of greed, and it is highly likely that there are yet more unsavoury stories to come from this quarter. Match-fixing by players in cricket matches is one of the latest to emerge, since cricket is a particularly easy game to arrange spot-fixing on (that is, bets on what happens within specified short sequences of play).[3] Several players have been found guilty of the practice, such as the Pakistani internationals Salman Butt and Mohammad Asif in 2011, both of whom were subsequently given bans by the cricketing authorities. Tennis and snooker are also coming under suspicion for the same reason, and several umpires have already been handed bans.[4] It is gamblers and gambling syndicates, unmistakably motivated by greed, who are the corrupting influence here, offering substantial financial inducements to players, and match officials, to draw them into fixing schemes. But the players have to be open to such approaches in order for these schemes to work, and it appears that quite a few of them were. It is now a case of watch this space to discover just how extensive the phenomenon turns out to be.

We can only note yet again how easily greed can take root in institutional contexts. It tends to elicit a very adverse reaction when we come up against instances of it in action, yet it does appear to be deeply rooted in our psychology, as we find out when entire institutions like FIFA are corrupted by it. When it comes to individuals, such as the disgraced cycling hero Lance Armstrong, it is not so much financial greed involved, as greed for the fame and public glory that follows on from sporting success. How else can we explain the determination of so many athletes to ignore all moral objections to doping in their quest for Olympic medals? They are driven by an apparently desperate need for fame, and while this drive can win approval as long as it is done fairly, the public can be very unforgiving when it finds it is drug-assisted, as Armstrong discovered.[5]

The most insidious aspect of scandals like these is the way that they combine to undermine public trust in both the athletes and their administrators. Whether it is match-fixing, spot-fixing or drug-enhanced performance that is brought to light, the credibility of results and world records is thrown seriously into question, rendering the whole exercise essentially meaningless, as sports fans no longer know what to believe or what is real. It is yet one more example of how greed can short-change the public.

9
THE ART OF GREED

Greed is a subject that has fascinated creative artists over the years, with misers and unscrupulous entrepreneurs providing painters, writers and filmmakers with a solid basis for social commentary. Dramatists, for example, have found greed, and particularly the antics of the miser, a source of considerable inspiration, both for tragic and comedic purposes, as in Shakespeare's *The Merchant of Venice* (1596–9), Ben Jonson's *Volpone* (1607) and Molière's *The Miser* (1668). In prose fiction, Scrooge in Charles Dickens's *A Christmas Carol* (1843) is one of the most famous such figures in modern times. In *Hard Times* (1854), the same author presents a caustic account of greed in the nineteenth-century factory-owner class, and its harsh impact on workers in a characteristic northern mill-town. Marxist authors have been predictably critical of greed, regarding it as the essence of the capitalist mentality, with Bertolt Brecht's *Mother Courage* (1939) showing how it can distort even the most fundamental of human values, such as the care of one's family.

Given the highly critical attitude of the Church towards avarice, it is not surprising that misers proved such a popular subject for painters in medieval and early modern times. *Avarice* (1507) is the title of a well-known work of Albrecht Dürer, featuring a haggard old woman greedily clutching a hoard of coins, and Hieronymus Bosch's *Death and the Miser* (c. 1485–90) constitutes a particularly striking treatment of the subject. The theme also crops up in the work of various other artists, such as Pieter Breugel the Elder, so its impact on the creative community is not hard to identify.

Unscrupulous businessmen and financiers feature prominently in films, with the character of Gordon Gekko in Oliver Stone's 1987 film *Wall Street* becoming iconic in that respect. Martin Scorsese's *The Wolf of Wall Street* (2013) continues that tradition on into the even more freewheeling and ruthless financial world of the twenty-first century, as does Adam McKay's *The Big Short* (2015). A notable treatment of the subject in earlier film history was *Greed* (1924), based on Frank Norris's novel *McTeague*, which was first published in 1899. The director Erich von Stroheim was clearly obsessed with the subject, producing a vastly overlength – especially by the standards of silent cinema – piece of work, several hours long (the exact figure varying depending on the commentator). The film exists now only in the much shorter version put out by its studio, who could see no market for it otherwise. How relevant its message is to a twenty-first-century audience is certainly well worth dwelling on here.

Christian European culture has always had an uneasy relationship with the Jews in its midst, and greed is only one of many anti-social traits they have been accused of over the centuries. Shylock is therefore in many ways a caricature, the Jewish moneylender willing to go to inhuman lengths in order to extract payment for his loans. Jews were often moneylenders and bankers in medieval and early modern Europe. The Christian Church disapproved strongly of the practice of usury; yet at the same time there was a growing market for loans as trade advanced, and the Jews stepped in to provide that service. There was at the least a certain amount of hypocrisy in Christian culture to condemn usury on the one hand, but for its adherents to become regular customers of usurers on the other (although as James Shapiro notes in *Shakespeare and the Jews*, attitudes towards usury were changing in Shakespeare's time, and English moneylenders were starting to make an appearance).[1] Jews played a critical role in the rise of the modern economic order in that respect, granting loans to enable the volume of trade to increase throughout Europe, and being instrumental in the establishment of the banking industry that came to underpin this. A character like Shylock is thus placed in the invidious position of being simultaneously a despised yet necessary element of European society at the time (particularly given the very high rates of interest Jewish moneylenders were reputed to charge), which puts his greed into a somewhat different perspective.

For Shylock to insist on his 'pound of flesh' in lieu of his loan being repaid, however, is to test any incipient sympathy the audience may feel for his precarious social situation as an outsider in Venetian society. He suffers harshly for making the demand, and it is undoubtedly an unreasonable one for him to have insisted upon, recalling widely disseminated tales in Shakespeare's time of the ritual murder of Christians by Jews (one of the things that makes '*The Merchant of Venice* so unsettling a comedy', for Shapiro).[2] But the Christians who punish Shylock hardly commend themselves to us either. They find a legal loophole and successfully exploit it when Portia points out in her defence of Antonio that Venetian law states that any 'alien' who threatens the life of a citizen (which fulfilment of the contract obviously would) is thereby subject to the following punishment:

> The party 'gainst the which he doth contrive
> Shall seize one-half his goods. The other half
> Comes to the privy coffer of the state,
> And the offender's life lies in the mercy
> Of the Duke only, 'gainst all other voice.[3]

The result is that Shylock is financially ruined as well as forced to convert to Christianity; an extremely cruel fate to inflict on him, robbing him of his ethnic identity as well as his means of existence. So we are entitled to ask, who is the greediest party by the end of the play? It could be argued that Shylock has been swindled, transformed from villain to victim, and that his opponents have been guilty of some very sharp practice which should put doubts in the audience's mind as to their morality. Alan Sinfield takes this line when he accuses the upper-class Venetians of being 'openly arrogant, scornful, snobbish, rich, and generally nasty' towards Shylock, going on to suggest how watching a performance of the play made him want to take the moneylender's side:

> For once, the stigmatized other seemed to have the drop on the rest of them: their prized mercantile and legal system, which was designed to keep the Jews in servility, had allowed him a loophole (as sometimes it must), and he was going to turn the tables. Of course, the Venetians were all for the quality of mercy now, since one of them was under threat. But I thought: Right on, Shylock, now's your chance, don't take any notice of their tricks, stick on in there and get your pound of flesh.[4]

Sinfield concedes this is 'a high-risk strategy', both for himself as a critic and for Shylock – presumably on the basis that moneylenders can only elicit so much sympathy, even when, as here, rendered into victims.[5] Yet Sinfield cannot suppress a certain admiration that at least Shylock has 'had a go' at taking on the establishment.[6] The moral we might draw from the play concerning greed is perhaps less straightforward than it might at first appear, even if, as Sinfield further notes of the night's experience, 'Some people in the audience were manifestly, and unpleasantly, delighted when Shylock was defeated.'[7]

Greed is what drives the character of Jonson's Volpone, and this is revealed instantly when he makes his entrance to begin the play: 'Good morning to the day / and, next, my gold! / Open the shrine, that I may see my saint.'[8] Volpone is obsessed by his wealth, and also by his devious method of increasing it through wheedling gifts out of those hoping to inherit his fortune, by holding out the prospect that he may name one of them as his beneficiary in his will:

> I have no wife, no parent, child, ally,
> To give my substance to; but whom I make,
> Must be my heir: and this makes men observe me.
> This draws new clients, daily, to my house,
> Women, and men, of every sex and age,
> That bring me presents, send me plate, coin, jewels,
> With hope, that when I die (which they expect
> Each greedy minute) it shall then return,
> Tenfold, upon them.[9]

Volpone is determined to exploit the greed of others to his own advantage, declaring himself 'content to coin 'em into profit'.[10] Volpone takes much pleasure in the 'sport' of conning others, and his success inflates his sense of self-worth to a ridiculous degree, leading him to think of himself as a cunning 'fox', able to outwit all and sundry by his wiles:

> Now, now, my clients
> Begin their visitation! Vulture, kite,
> Raven, and gor-crow, all my birds of prey,
> That think me turning carcass, now they come;
> I am not for 'em yet.[11]

He is not as wily as he thinks, however, as his servant Mosca (who proudly describes himself as a 'parasite') is scheming away behind his back, with several equally dubious associates, to swindle him in turn. No one can be trusted around riches, it would seem.

Volpone eventually receives his comeuppance, being banished to a monastery by the authorities and, like Shylock, having his wealth confiscated. Mosca, too, is caught out, and sentenced to spend the rest of his life as a galley slave. Whether their respective fates will act as a warning to others, and excise greed from Venetian society altogether, has to be a doubtful prospect. Volpone and Mosca may have been removed from the scene, but the former's many greedy 'clients', his 'birds of prey', are still in circulation, most likely hunting for new opportunities to become rich in a hurry. Avarice seems to be the default character trait in this world, and riches exert an irresistible pull.

Molière's *The Miser* presents us with the even more ridiculous figure of Harpagon, whose greed leads to all kinds of family problems, not least that despite his advanced age he is intent on marrying the young woman with whom his son is in love. Harpagon has made his fortune by lending money out at very high rates, and he worships it no less than Volpone does his gold. In this respect, he concludes the play's action in entirely appropriate fashion, when he takes his leave of the rest of the company by making it clear where his real interest will always lie: 'And let me go and see my beloved cash box again.'[12] He is notoriously mean in using any of his riches: his servants are forced to go around in rags; his son and daughter are denied any money of their own (Harpagon repeatedly asserting that he has none), and are treated as little better than possessions. Much against their wishes, Harpagon plans to marry them off for money; his son to a rich widow and his daughter to a wealthy fifty-year-old acquaintance of his. The main selling point for his daughter's intended, as Harpagon sees it, is that the match comes with 'a special, a unique advantage. He is willing to take her – without dowry.'[13] As his daughter's true lover, Valère, pointedly remarks of Harpagon, when it comes to money, 'you know that on this issue there is nothing good one can say of him.'[14]

Molière mines the comic potential of Harpagon's outrageously miserly and avaricious behaviour to good effect, as when he insists on searching his son's valet, La Flèche, before allowing him to leave the house, convinced that anyone who has been left there on his own, even for just a short while, must have stolen something. He simply cannot believe that everyone else is not as avaricious as he is, assuming that it is the defining characteristic of human nature. Just how unscrupulously avaricious he is capable of being is revealed at one point when he agrees to lend money to an unknown young man, whose case is being pressed by his agent, only if he will agree to terms of 25.5 per cent interest, and receiving some of the loan in goods rather than actual cash. When the unknown young man turns out to be Harpagon's son, Cléante, the latter is if anything the more shocked of the two, accusing his father of 'outdoing anything the most notorious usurers ever invented in the way of scandalous interest.'[15]

After a series of mix-ups and misunderstandings of the sort one would expect to find in a farcical comedy, the love tangle is eventually resolved and the way is cleared for Harpagon's son and daughter to marry their true loves. But Harpagon ensures that he does not have to pay anything towards the respective weddings, and his sustained meanness is in sharp contrast to the good humour of the rest of the cast as the tale is brought to a happy conclusion. Although both Shylock and Volpone are punished for their greed, Harpagon gets away scot-free (except for losing out romantically, preferable in his eyes to losing any of his money), which is the more likely outcome in real life too. The banks and traders involved in the credit crash generally got away with it, prosecutions being few and far between for all the public uproar about their behaviour; tax evasion, too, remains a fairly simple procedure for the corporate world to arrange. The financially greedy tend to be very adept at protecting themselves.

Brecht's play *Mother Courage* is set during the Thirty Years War of seventeenth-century Europe, and explores how greed can even overcome the ties between a mother and her children. Mother Courage's overriding concern is trade, and she has become parasitic upon the armies marauding across the continent, recognizing the opportunities that war offers for financial gain (as the business sector continues to do in our own day). As she bluntly puts it:

To hear the big chaps talk, they wage war from fear of God and for all things bright and beautiful, but just look into it, and you'll see they're not so silly: they want a good profit out of it, or else the little chaps like you and me wouldn't back 'em up.[16]

Morals in Mother Courage's case have been completely subordinated to the drive to obtain wealth, for Brecht a standard failing of capitalists at all times and places. Any compassion that Mother Courage may once have felt for others is suppressed by the business impulse, and it has become her primary reason for existence, to be pursued to the bitter end. In fact, by the play's conclusion it has cost her the lives of her children, and Brecht expects us to recognize just how culpable Mother Courage is – and just how culpable the system is that she represents. It is capitalism that is the villain here, and we are urged to note how it can destroy both personal morality and the social bond. Hence Mother Courage's comments in the aftermath of the death of the last of her children, Kattrin: 'I hope I can pull the wagon by myself. Yes, I'll manage, there's not much in it now. I must start up again in business.'[17] Brecht did not want the audience to feel pity for the character at this point, although audiences very often do (another 'high-risk strategy' perhaps), and performances in the English-speaking world can play up to this expectation. It is the corrupting power of the commercial instinct that he is concerned to impress on the audience, and Mother Courage is to be censured for allowing this to dominate her life so comprehensively. As Brecht sees it, that instinct is a dehumanizing force.

Dickens's Scrooge is one of the most memorably mean-spirited characters in fiction, and he has made a strong impact on the public imagination. Unlike most of the treatments of the subject, *A Christmas Carol* is brought to a happy ending, with Scrooge renouncing his miserly ways in a complete reversal of his character, being transformed, somewhat improbably from the ogre he had become, into a kind-hearted benefactor spreading largesse around him with a beaming countenance (something that the popular usage of his name nowadays passes over). Before his transformation, however, Scrooge is a classic miser, reluctant to part with any of his money at all and begrudging the poor wages that he pays to his clerk, Bob Cratchit, whom he keeps hard at work for long hours in a barely heated office:

> Oh! but he was a tight-fisted hand at the grindstone. Scrooge! a squeezing, wrenching, grasping, scraping, clutching, covetous old sinner! Hard and sharp as flint, from which no steel had ever struck out generous fire; secret, and self-contained, and solitary as an oyster.[18]

Cratchit is struggling to keep his family, including his crippled son 'Tiny Tim', on the small salary he earns. As a result the family is collectively facing the bleakest of Christmases, until Scrooge turns up at his office on Christmas morning in his changed character, brought on by a nightmare full of ghastly spirits warning him to repent of his evil ways. Told by Scrooge that he is about to increase his salary, Cratchit's immediate reaction is to think that Scrooge must have gone mad: 'Bob trembled, and got a little nearer to the ruler. He had a momentary idea of knocking Scrooge down with it, holding him, and calling to the people in the court for help and a strait-waistcoat.'[19] This is, after all, someone who on Christmas Eve the day before flatly refused to make a donation to a charitable fund set up to help the poor at Christmas, 'in want of common necessaries', remarking tetchily instead that, 'I don't make merry myself at Christmas and I can't afford to make idle people merry.'[20] The greedy individual is in this case brought to a full realization of the effect of his greed on others, and comes to recognize the need to repent – not a lesson to be repeated in the fiction of Frank Norris. Repentance on the lines of Scrooge is a rare phenomenon in the business world.

Hard Times presents us with greed in the more institutionalized form of the grasping factory owners of the fictional northern
town of Coketown. Here greed has become a way of life, the basis
on which the town operates. The Coketown industrialists are
implacable in their opposition to the demands of their workforce,
determined to pay them as little as they can get away with, even if
it leaves the workers in dire poverty and at times close to starvation
– particularly during times of economic slow-down (and these were
common during the period). It is only too true a picture of how
the social system worked in a mid-nineteenth-century England,
where industrialization was in full spate, with little control over
how it was developing. Profit is the owners' only concern, and
they are single-minded and totally hard-hearted about how they
accumulate it, regarding their workers with open contempt as 'a
bad lot altogether', unworthy of any better treatment.[21] Were these
employers transported to the twenty-first century, they would
only too happily take to a culture of zero-hours contracts and
employment casualization, not to mention tax avoidance.

The luxurious lifestyle of the owners is in stark contrast to the
subsistence existence eked out by their employees. Dickens lays
the irony on thick in describing this, his tone clearly communi-
cating how little respect he has for the factory-owners as well as
his innate sympathy for the plight of their unfortunate workers.
Life for the latter is pretty grim all round, and they are fated to
perform deadeningly monotonous work for long hours in a dark
and depressing industrial landscape, with little to look forward to;
but, as the author points out:

> These attributes of Coketown were in the main inseparable
> from the work by which it was sustained; against them
> were to be set off, comforts of life which found their way
> all over the world, and elegancies of life which made, we
> will not ask how much of the fine lady, who could scarcely
> bear to hear the place mentioned.[22]

There is little sign of any significant 'trickle down' (as neoliberal economists would describe it) of the profits of manufacturing on view here. The rich remain oblivious, deliberately so, to the human cost of their luxuries, to the sheer misery and desperation involved in the production of their many 'comforts' and 'elegancies', or to the 'hard times' these are inflicting on those lower down the socioeconomic scale. Sadly we go on doing so in the West with regards to the pay and conditions of the workforce in the developing world who are employed to produce our own 'comforts' and 'elegancies'. Occasionally these make news – if some large-scale accident occurs because of poor health and safety provision in a factory, for example – but the system rarely changes much afterwards. In this respect, *Hard Times* remains a very relevant work for twenty-first-century readers. We are just as capable of taking advantage of an unfair system.

In the largely non-unionized times in which *Hard Times* is set, the factory hands are completely at the mercy of their employers, who exhibit precious little in the way of social conscience, being solely concerned with building up their personal fortunes for themselves and their families. Once again the parallels with today are obvious. And it is worth noting that annual profit margins in industry in Dickens's day could be massive in percentage terms (well into double, and even three figures on occasion), making it all the more reprehensible to see the character that developed in this setting: one self-interested to an almost inhuman degree. The attitude of the employers towards the working class is either contemptuous or, at best, patronizing, and they show little interest in the workers other than their ability to work as directed and make profits for others to enjoy. Coketown's education system is primarily designed to produce the next generation of workers, who will be indoctrinated to accept their expected role in life uncomplainingly and not to question the status quo. Their employers' greed for profits is simply to be regarded as the natural order of things, and the luxurious lifestyle they lead is taken to signal their greater social value. It is precisely this system, and the ideology that lies behind it, that so incensed Marx and galvanized him into producing his monumental critique against capitalism.

Frank Norris's novel *McTeague* (1899) is little read these days, but it did have its moment of fame, being memorably adapted for the screen by Erich von Stroheim in 1924. For all its flaws (latent anti-Semitism and more than a suggestion of misogyny), it deserves more recognition than it currently receives, constituting a trenchant indictment of the underlying value system in American life that continues to resonate right into our own time. Von Stroheim correctly identified the work's main focus in the title he chose for the film, now an acknowledged classic of silent cinema, *Greed*. Norris finds greed everywhere in late nineteenth-century American life. All of his main characters eventually succumb to its lure, which proves stronger than any of the ties of social relations. Friendship, love, marriage, family: none of these is protection against greed's insidious effects. Brecht would have been in full agreement with the sentiments. Overall *McTeague* paints a very uncomplimentary picture of American culture, where it apparently takes precious little prompting for greed to start displaying itself in any individual. The setting of San Francisco helps to intensify the impact of the theme, since it was a city that had sprung up from the gold rush of the mid-nineteenth century, only a few decades before Norris wrote the novel. It could reasonably be described as a city founded on human greed. McTeague himself is first pictured working as a miner, an occupation that he is to return to in the latter stages of the novel.

The novel catches America at a particularly interesting point in its history, just as it had passed its frontier days. It is still a rough-and-ready society, but a rapidly developing one, with all its inhabitants trying to cash in on its growing economic prosperity. The nation's value system is firmly based around money, and no one appears to be questioning the negative effect this is having on both public and personal morality. Thomas Carlyle had observed in the earlier days of the Industrial Revolution in England that 'the cash nexus' had become the new basis of human relations, and it certainly appears to be that way in Norris's San Francisco.[23] Personal greed is always lurking just under the surface of every individual, awaiting the chance to reveal itself. McTeague's girlfriend, then wife, Trina, becomes the most prominent symbol of this after she wins $5,000 in a lottery, a very substantial sum for the time. Trina cannot bear to touch any of the money, and soon turns into a full-scale miser, also secretly hoarding whatever she can save from the housekeeping money she receives from McTeague. Whenever McTeague makes a request for money from her, she lies as to the amount she has, claiming there is far less in her savings than he thinks, and utterly refusing to break into the lottery winnings.

Although aware of how her character is changing from her carefree girlhood days, Trina finds it all too easy to rationalize her behaviour: "'I didn't use to be so stingy," she told herself. "Since I won in the lottery I've become a regular little miser. It's growing on me, but never mind, it's a good fault, and anyhow, I can't help it."[24] Sadly this seems to be true of all Norris's main characters, who also feel they just 'can't help it' when money comes on the scene: at that point anyone is capable of being consumed by greed, and the impulse is rarely fought against or overcome for any great length of time. There is notably little in the way of love or affection on display between the characters; instead, relationships seem to revolve almost entirely around the 'cash nexus'. Norris's characters are more concerned about their own welfare, and most particularly their financial welfare, than that of others, no matter how close a relationship they might have to any of them.

A parallel plot demonstrating the psychological progress of greed in the individual is found in the story of the Jewish junkshop owner Zerkow and the rather simple-minded Mexican cleaning woman Maria Macapa. Maria keeps regaling everyone she knows with a tale, almost certainly a fantasy, of how her family had owned a large dinner service – 'more than a hundred pieces', as she boasts – made out of pure gold.[25] No one really believes her except Zerkow who cannot hear enough of the story, gold being an obsession of his: 'It was his dream, his passion: . . . The glint of it was constantly in his eyes; the jangle of it sang forever in his ears as the jingling of cymbals.'[26] Their relationship develops as Maria brings him the odds and ends she has picked up to sell for spare cash, including, all too symbolically, gold fillings which she has stolen from McTeague's dental surgery. These alone are enough to draw Zerkow to her, and he invariably seizes hold of them greedily, delighted to get his hands on gold of any kind. So obsessed does Zerkow become with Maria's descriptions of her family's supposed riches that he marries her, feeling that this is bound to bring him closer to possession of the service, convinced that Maria really does know where it is hidden away and that eventually she will reveal the secret to him. He is a character of whom the author notes: 'It was impossible to look at Zerkow and not know instantly that greed – inordinate, insatiable greed – was the dominant passion of the man.'[27]

There is a definitely anti-Semitic cast to Zerkow's characterization, with various asides by the author suggesting that his conduct is typical of his race, and this will grate with a modern audience. In fact, Zerkow proves to be no more greedy than the other main characters. Even when his obsession spurs him on to murder Maria at her refusal to reveal the location of the gold plates (after she has started to deny the truth of the tale herself), this is paralleled by McTeague's behaviour in murdering Trina to lay his hands, finally, on the lottery money that she so jealously guards. The novel ultimately shows that greed can drive anyone, regardless of their ethnic background, to desperate acts. If the opportunity presents itself then the trait will swiftly rise to the surface. Overall it is a damning comment on human nature.

Marcus Schouler, McTeague's best friend as the narrative opens, is another who falls victim to greed's distorting influence. When we first meet him he is Trina's boyfriend, a fairly happy-go-lucky character, and the pair are expected to marry at some future point. However, McTeague is instantly smitten with Trina when Marcus brings her into his surgery for treatment, and he confesses his plight to Marcus, who offers to step aside in favour of his friend. All very gallant it would seem, but it is soon revealed that Marcus is somewhat less than passionate in his feelings towards Trina, and not overly concerned at giving up the relationship (the film version treats this far more sentimentally than the book does, as an expression of male friendship). Yet after Trina's lottery win Marcus's attitude changes dramatically to one of deep resentment at having lost access to the money, and from then onwards he harbours a grudge against McTeague, even throwing a knife at him when they have a quarrel in a bar. He never forgives McTeague completely, and their duel to the death in the narrative's closing stages has an air of inevitability about it. This is all despite the fact that when Marcus first appears he is prone to delivering socialist tirades to all and sundry after a few drinks:

> 'It's the capitalists that's ruining the cause of labor,' shouted Marcus, banging the table with his fist till the beer glasses danced; 'white-livered drones, traitors, with their livers white as snow, eatun the bread of widows and orphuns; there's where the evil lies.'[28]

Greed runs deeper in human psychology than even political beliefs.

Trina's miserliness becomes more and more of an issue as she and McTeague fall on hard times when he is barred from practising dentistry for lacking the appropriate professional qualifications (he picked up the trade while working as the assistant of a charlatan travelling dentist for several years). Both McTeague and Trina blame Marcus for being the one to inform the authorities of his lack of qualifications, further inflaming the feud between them. Despite their growing hardship as McTeague fails to find any suitable alternative long-term employment, Trina steadfastly refuses to release any of the lottery winnings to ease their situation. Instead, she becomes ever more intent on adding to her secret personal savings by scrimping on the housekeeping – even going to the length of cheating McTeague out of his correct change when she is buying food. McTeague grows increasingly exasperated by her stinginess and their relationship slowly unravels, with McTeague sliding into alcoholism and Trina coming to despise, and also fear, him. Physical violence becomes his method of extorting what small amounts of money from Trina he can, and he frequently resorts to biting her hands so badly that eventually she has to have some fingers amputated. This sets the tone for the even more violent episodes that are to follow.

The narrative's final scene is set in Death Valley, where McTeague has fled to escape being prosecuted for Trina's brutal murder. It seems an appropriately stark setting, human emotions being reduced to their most elemental in the barren desert landscape. Marcus, who has moved down near the area to become a rancher, catches sight of a wanted poster for McTeague, and talks himself into the pursuing posse being led by a local sheriff. When the posse decides against crossing Death Valley, choosing to circle around it instead, Marcus foolhardily sets out on his own, determined to catch McTeague single-handedly. His resentment at McTeague having, as he thinks of it, stolen 'his' money by the act of marrying Trina, has festered over the years and revenge is now the only thing on his mind. From then on the chase becomes a chapter of tragic errors, with reason having long since gone out of the window as far as both men are concerned. After Marcus captures McTeague, they are marooned out in the desert in blistering heat, with no waterholes anywhere nearby. When McTeague's horse turns skittish through eating poisonous locoweed, they are forced to shoot it to stop it galloping away, and in doing so burst the water containers hanging on its flanks, meaning they no longer have any water at all left between them. The struggle that ensues ends with McTeague bludgeoning Marcus to death, but not before

Marcus succeeds in handcuffing himself to McTeague, leaving him unable to get away. Marcus has gained his revenge, but at the expense of his own life. Greed has brought both characters to a bad end, as it has Trina, and Zerkow, who is found drowned in the bay shortly after Maria's murder.

The film itself has a chequered history, having been drastically cut by the studio from the director's original version. When it was eventually released, it was around the two-hour mark, much to the director's displeasure, Von Stroheim having remained particularly faithful to the narrative of the novel. He clearly felt quite passionate about the book, and seemed reluctant to cut anything that he had filmed. Whereas nowadays that might have made it a good bet for a multi-part project (such as *The Lord of the Rings* trilogy) or television series, that was not the way the film world operated in the silent era. *Greed* made little impression at the box office, and more or less disappeared until interest was revived in it by later generations of film historians, many of whom now feel it is arguably the greatest ever American silent film, and a trenchant account of the country's obsession with money. Unfortunately much of Von Stroheim's original footage was never found (it was probably destroyed), and even though it now exists in a lovingly restored four-hour version, much of that is made up of stills interspersed by chunks of text taken from the novel to bridge all that is left from the studio's actual release.

One of the most effective additions the film makes to the book's scenes is a recurrent shot of hands turning a pile of gold pieces over and over, their owners clearly entranced at having so much wealth right there at their fingertips. It is the dream of so many of the characters, particularly Trina, who periodically communes with her own savings in just this manner. The message is clear: once greed takes root in your character then it soon comes to dominate your outlook and actions, and the message is that it can happen to anyone. All of us have the capability to be greedy; it lies latent within our psychology, only waiting for the right opportunity to arise.

The Death Valley scenes are particularly effective on film, the harsh light and inhuman desolation of the desert coming across strongly. This is human life at its most basic, a revenge tragedy played out in an unforgiving landscape that puts survival severely at risk, and that neither character can manage to conquer. Death is the only possible outcome, as both characters are made to pay the ultimate penalty for their sins. 'Inordinate, insatiable greed' proves to be their downfall too, as it was with Trina and Zerkow.

There was an even earlier version of the novel made for the silent screen, entitled *Life's Whirlpool* (1916), but this has now been lost. Clearly the story caught the imagination of the time. And just to indicate that it can still inspire interest, more recently, in 1992, *McTeague* was adapted for the opera stage by the American composer William Bolcom.

Despite its faults, *McTeague* is a very powerful critique of the American value system, and it still has something of significance to say to us today. There does seem to be something wrong with a system in which self-interest is so rife, and where it is cultivated to such an extent. As the critic Eric Solomon remarks, '*McTeague* is not the Great American Novel but a wonderfully interesting and stimulating one' all the same – a guarded recommendation, perhaps – but Norris is still worth reading.[29] He believes there is something very rotten at the heart of American capitalism, and it is a theme that he returns to in the novel that follows *McTeague*, *The Octopus: A Story of California*. This was planned as part of a trilogy to be called *Wheat*, which Norris died before he could finish, only getting as far as the second part, *The Pit: A Story of Chicago* (the last instalment was to have been set in Europe, the American wheat crop's main destination). Once again it is human greed that comes under the microscope, the 'inordinate, insatiable greed' that to Norris is the dark secret of the American soul. For Norris, this greed finds its most potent expression in the organized forces of the corporate world, symbolized in the novel by the 'octopus' of the railway companies, whose tentacles spread everywhere, crushing the life out of all those who lie in its path. Indeed, as so many of the work's characters are to discover, to take a stand against the railway 'octopus' is to put your life at risk. The railway brooks no resistance at all to its will, and has huge resources at its command: 'the inexhaustible coffers of a mighty organisation'.[30]

The Octopus is a sprawling novel with several interlinked plots working their way through the narrative, often at a very leisurely pace. It is an uneven work, awkwardly juxtaposing romanticized views of the West with a recognition of the conflicting forces that its exploitation has set in motion: the West, a microcosm of the rest of the United States, is rapidly turning into a battlefield. In the novel's opening stages, the poet Presley is pictured struggling with the growing impact that those conflicting forces are having on the rural California to which he has become so attached:

> He had set himself the task of giving true, absolutely true, poetical expression to the life of the ranch, and yet, again and again, he brought up against the railroad, that stubborn iron barrier against which his romance shattered itself to froth and disintegrated, flying spume.[31]

The wheat farmers who form the focus of the story vary in terms of the size of their holdings. Some of the ranches are huge, filling up the whole horizon as viewed by the proud owners from their home-stead, which can often be quite palatial in appearance, while others are much smaller in scale. But not even the biggest of them has the power to stand up to the railroad and its agents for long. Almost all the main farming characters end up either dead or financially ruined, crushed by the railroad's cruel policies, and it is a sad tale overall – especially when you consider that almost all of the villainous characters escape unscathed. The only ultimate winner is organized capital, and it has absolutely no social conscience; its only concern is squeezing the last drop of profit it can from the consumer, and it is relentless in its methods. In our own day, supermarket chains are often criticized for treating their suppliers in just such a harsh fashion, driving down the latter's profit margins to bump up their own.

Given the desperate fate of the farming community, which is effectively demolished by the railroad company's sheer ruthlessness, it is more than a little surprising that Norris chooses to end the novel on an upbeat note:

> Falseness dies; injustice and oppression in the end of everything fade and vanish away. Greed, cruelty, selfishness, and inhumanity are short-lived; the individual suffers, but the race goes on. . . . The larger view always and through all shams, all wickednesses, discovers the Truth that will, in the end, prevail, and all things, surely, inevitably, resistlessly work together for good.[32]

There is little in Norris's epic tale of woe to merit such an optimistic conclusion, however, and it comes across as just so much wishful thinking. We are left instead to contemplate the resounding triumph of 'the soulless Force, the iron-hearted Power, the monster, the Colossus, the Octopus'.[33] How the Octopus can be countered remains a mystery, and to be told that life nevertheless goes on provides precious little comfort. Norris's optimism in the face of all evidence to the contrary might be regarded as only too characteristic of American culture: the belief that the nation's ideals will ultimately prevail such that everyone will benefit from its resulting economic success. If greed really is as entrenched in the American character as Norris's work insists, then this would seem to be something of a forlorn hope. His work implies that greed will win out, and greed is always socially divisive. Looking around in our own day, there is no indication that the corporate forces are any less powerful than they were in Norris's, nor any more motivated by a sense of social conscience. The 'shareholder defence' can always be trotted out to justify almost any action that increases profits. Profit comes before people in this context.

The Pit continues Norris's exploration into the subject of greed, this time focusing on commodities trading in the wheat market in Chicago around the turn of the twentieth century. The fate of the wheat farmers passes entirely out of their own hands at this stage, as again we are plunged into a world of grasping individuals doing their utmost to improve their own economic situation without regard for the effect their actions may have on others, spurred on by a greed that appears to be one of the great driving forces of the American marketplace. Market speculation tends to bring some of the worst aspects of human nature to the surface. The speculators are always on the lookout for an opportunity to make a killing, and if it is at the expense of their fellow human beings then so much the better. Personal gain is the overriding concern, whether arrived at by fair means or foul.

As in *The Octopus*, the narrative of *The Pit* is conceived of on a grand scale as a clash between very different ways of life: the world of money versus the world of art, individual entrepreneurial drive versus social spirit, tradition versus the new ruthless capitalist order. Norris can, however, appreciate how the marketplace can cast its spell over us, describing how one of his protagonists, Laura Dearborn, who is far more disposed towards the world of art than trade, reacts to being driven through Chicago's commercial area late at night:

> Suddenly the meaning and significance of it all dawned upon Laura. The Great Grey City, brooking no rival, imposed its dominion upon a reach of country larger than many a kingdom of the Old World ... Here, of all her cities, throbbed the true life – the true power and spirit of America; gigantic, crude with the crudity of its youth, disdaining rivalry ... Laura, her eyes dizzied, her ears stunned, watched tirelessly.[34]

The Octopus is at work once more, as it seems to be throughout the whole country. It is a force from which there is no real escape, effortlessly generating greed in every walk of life.

Unfortunately, very few can resist the lure of the Octopus. One of the novel's main characters, Curtis Jadwin, a market speculator who is later to become Laura's husband, provides a very cautionary tale in this respect. He is a property owner who occasionally dabbles in speculation, but usually quite circumspectly, well aware of how easy it is to be sucked into the market on such a scale that your whole fortune is placed at risk. Jadwin has only to visit the city's Board of Trade to observe the pathetic state of some once-powerful but now ruined speculators, hanging around pretending that they are still part of the commodities' trading scene even though they no longer have the wherewithal to make deals or investments. Jadwin is offered a chance by his broker, Sam Gretry, to corner the market in wheat for a short period, a move which potentially could bring them both a very quick, and very large, windfall. Jadwin initially declines, but it does not take much for the broker to persuade him to take a chance after all and to part with a substantial sum of money in order to put together the necessary trades. It is not as if Jadwin really needs more money. At the age of 35 he is already a wealthy man, having worked his way up from a humble beginning, in the time-honoured American fashion. Yet the opportunity to put one over on his business competitors proves just too tempting – it almost always does for speculators.

The deal proves a success, yet a friend of Jadwin's, Charles Creswell, who is an older and wiser hand in the trading business, sounds a disapproving note:

> I'm not going to congratulate you . . . As far as that's concerned, I would rather you had lost than won – if it would have kept you out of the Pit [the trading floor of the Chicago Board of Trade] for good. You're cocky now. I know – good Lord, don't I know. I had my share of it. I know how a man gets drawn into this speculating game.[35]

But it proves too late to issue warnings to Jadwin; he has already been drawn into the game. Before too long he is playing it for really big stakes, putting up larger and larger amounts of his personal fortune as collateral for the deals he is making, taking greater and greater risks in consequence. He soon reaches the stage where he cannot imagine life without speculation to hold his interest. It is the old familiar story of Norris's world: the greed impulse strikes again, and strikes hard. You need only succumb to its lure once, and greed so easily becomes addictive, gradually taking over your whole life if you are not careful. Jadwin's tragedy is that he begins to think of himself as a 'Master of the Universe', and he becomes obsessed with 'cornering the market'. The outcome is only too predictable: he really does corner the market, and with that has the power to drive the cost of wheat up to whatever level he chooses. The problem is that he becomes so greedy that he cannot prevent himself from continuing to do so, pushing the trading price of wheat to such a high level that eventually the market turns on him. Once unleashed, the greed impulse can never be satisfied; whatever it achieves can never be enough. Jadwin proves to be a classic example of greed's character-destroying power, and of the overreaching figure who does not know when to stop. As in *McTeague*, greed also wreaks havoc with his personal life, alienating his wife and jeopardizing his marriage.

Exactly how dangerous the greed impulse can be in a wider social sense is particularly well captured by Norris in the diatribe that Creswell subsequently delivers against the whole system of market speculation:

> They call it buying and selling ... But it is simply betting. Betting on the condition of the market weeks, even months, in advance. You bet wheat goes up. I bet it goes down ... Think of it, the food of hundreds and hundreds of thousands of people just at the mercy of a few men down there on the Board of Trade. They make the price. They say just how much the peasant shall pay for his loaf of bread. If he can't pay the price he simply starves.[36]

There is much more in the same vein, and at times like this Norris reveals a powerful ability to bring out capitalism's deficiencies (hidden beneath the notion of economic progress), and why so many of us feel a distinct sense of unease about the underlying anarchy of the market system. It is all the more ironic and telling, therefore, that Creswell of all people is persuaded to join the clique that brings Jadwin down. Once a speculator, always a speculator, it would seem – even when you realize what is wrong with the system. He suffers from his decision, however, finding himself ruined before Jadwin's eventual fall, and commits suicide to escape the ignominy this brings.

Norris can come across as proto-communist when he moves into his stride on the issue of greed, and very much at variance with the prevailing business ethic in the u.s., then and now. The stock market is indeed based on betting (although it will rarely be described that way by its defenders), and behind that lies the desire to get something for nothing, regardless of how it may affect the welfare of others. Greed overrides social conscience and, as Norris repeatedly makes clear in his fiction, some will always suffer when egocentricity is given free rein in this manner: first, the close relations of the greedy individual, and in time the wider society beyond that. It is a system we still labour under in our own day, and its sheer complexity now offers even more opportunities for greedy individuals to indulge their self-interest and enrich themselves, to the ultimate detriment of countless others further down the line. Those who benefit, of course, simply ignore this uncomfortable fact, seeing themselves instead as agents of economic growth. Norris cuts through that self-serving notion to reveal the antisocial nature of most market trading, inspired not by a sense of altruism but by much darker personal motives. At his best, Norris is an impressive social critic.

We can only wonder how Norris would have developed as a writer had he not died at the young age of 32, but he did seem to be turning into one of the most penetrating critics of the American way of life, and particularly of the way that greed has infiltrated itself into the very fabric of the nation's culture. Greed is presented as the unavoidable consequence of the modern marketplace and the forces that propel it. As far as Norris is concerned, America's economic success comes at a considerable sociological and psychological cost, and few can escape its ramifications. Many recent commentators on America's socioeconomic development are inclined to agree with this overall pessimistic assessment. George Packer, for example, in his acclaimed sociological study *The Unwinding: An Inner History of the New America* identifies greed for wealth as America's 'default force', with 'organized money' driving it along relentlessly.[37] The ruthless laissez-faire capitalism of Norris's day is matched by the equally ruthless neoliberalism of our own, both of them capable of bringing out some of the worst aspects of human nature. (The humbling of Greece in 2015 after its attempt to escape from the austerity politics imposed on it by its creditors in the European Union is a sharp reminder of just how ruthless neoliberals in power can be. In effect, a whole nation was held to ransom by its creditors, who ganged up on the country in a very unsavoury fashion that was not pleasant to observe.) As Packer recounts, communities can be destroyed and individual lives wrecked, if organized money decides it will be to its financial advantage to outsource production to cheaper developing countries – shareholders will expect no less. Much heavy industry has vanished from the West in consequence, and with it a whole way of life that was holding many communities together. 'Octopus' becomes a very apt metaphor to apply to the workings of the shareholder system, which is the norm for commercial activity across the globe.

Norris is an interesting but flawed author, worth reading for his themes rather than his prose style (which admittedly can be ponderous), and that is the reason I have gone into his work at some length. Notwithstanding the questionable aspects of his fiction – the anti-Semitism and misogyny can be hard for a modern audience to forgive – he registers nevertheless as an immensely astute social critic of the American scene, and his jaundiced view of his culture and the role that greed has come to play in its development echoes through the years. It is certainly there in the figure of Oliver Stone's Gordon Gekko, whose name has become a byword for financial greed since the release of the director's film *Wall Street* in 1987.

For Stone, Gekko represents everything that is wrong with America's financial sector, its toxic combination of greed and amorality in a world seemingly hermetically sealed from everyday considerations. Events since have shown us just how toxic it can be. Gekko is absolutely ruthless in his methods, unconcerned at the damage to others' lives that activities such as asset-stripping of companies – a speciality of his – can cause. If he seems to be an overblown caricature, and he does come across as more than something of a monster, it is not so difficult to find real-life equivalents in the financial and business worlds. Gekko is obsessed with the stock market and the deals he has pulled off over the years; in fact he can talk about little else than stocks and money. He has a very one-dimensional view of the world, right down to judging people almost purely on their wealth and market trading acumen: they are either useful to him in his schemes or they are to be quickly discarded. One protégé of his, Bud Fox, is eventually arrested for insider trading, having been prompted into it in the first place by Gekko, who has absolutely no regard for stock market regulations. In his view, you should take advantage of whatever gives you an edge on your competitors, legal or otherwise, and this is a view shared by many of his real-life counterparts. Insider trading is just a fact of life in the stock market, and the temptation to make a quick windfall by engaging in it all too frequently proves stronger than the fear of arrest and indictment.

Martin Scorsese's *The Wolf of Wall Street* (2013), adapted from Jordan Belfort's real-life memoir of his career as a New York investment company owner, paints a lurid picture of the excesses that greed can lead to, its characters squandering their stock market gains on wild parties and drug-taking on an epic scale.[38] Belfort's exploits make Gekko's seem tame by comparison, and the film pictures a world of debauchery and greed that outdoes even Brecht's Marxist-prejudiced vision of America. Belfort's firm, using the hardest of hard-sell techniques, treats investors as little more than prey, and the staff's only interest lies in accumulating their personal commissions from sales, rewards that soon run into ludicrous figures. The stocks they are selling are more often than not worthless, but such is the tenor of the times that would-be investors respond readily to the sales pitch which promises that these particular stocks represent their golden opportunity to get rich quick. Greed is everywhere in a society that appears to regard becoming rich as every individual's natural right, and in that respect firms like Belfort's had a very receptive clientele to work on; people really do want to believe what they are told. Nor is Belfort to be considered an isolated case of bad behaviour; Seth Freedman, for example, reminiscing on his career as a City trader in London, admits: 'I was caught in an endless loop . . . I went to work, made money, spent it on drink, drugs and other pursuits, struggled into work again the next day.'[39]

Belfort is eventually arrested by the FBI for securities fraud, but agrees to cooperate with the authorities and provide inside details as to exactly what was going on in his firm, and to name everyone connected with his crooked schemes. His punishment is a relatively light sentence, and he only spends 22 months in jail before an early release – fairly generous treatment, given the extent of the fraud he perpetrated. The film's makers regard it as a 'cautionary tale', but it is worth noting that Belfort sold the film rights to his book for a large sum, and is now making a very good living as a motivational speaker on the international circuit. Crime, apparently, does pay.

The 2015 film *The Big Short* is based on Michael Lewis's book of the same name. It traces the market adventures of a group of real-life traders who were so confident that a major crash was looming that they started speculating on that basis, betting that the banking system would fail because of the bad (that is, subprime mortgage) loans it had made. Lewis's book is an eye-opening exposé on how the traders worked this out and successfully exploited the situation, although in a way the details are less important than the underlying attitudes that it reveals to be at work. The notion that failure is simply to be regarded as an interesting business opportunity will most likely baffle those of us who do not play the market. It requires us to get our head around the fact that from an investing standpoint, failure can be a good thing, and it can even lead to substantial financial gains for those smart enough to manipulate it. Three such traders formed a company called Cornwall Capital in 2002, and as Lewis notes, its 'bet against subprime mortgage bonds had quadrupled its capital, from a bit more than $30 million to $135 million', as the market collapsed.[40] I suspect that the majority of us probably thought that the key to investing was to identify successful performance, not poor, and will find the whole episode more than a little confusing – not to say worrying. It is hard to know whether to classify those involved as villains or simply very astute operators. Whatever the decision, their activities do make for a dramatic scenario.

In the event, failure proved to be a very good thing indeed for this particular group, who proceeded to make a great deal of money out of the 2007–8 market crash, proving that greed is never lacking in ingenuity. Given that the system was only rescued from total collapse by various Western governments pumping in public money on an unprecedented scale (think trillions of dollars), we are left yet again to marvel at the sheer shamelessness of the financial world and its operators. As long as the latter benefit they will push on with their speculating, whether it is for the good of the system or not; their interest will be focused only on the gains to be made. Yet the impact of such films and books on the popular consciousness indicates just how fascinating we continue to find depictions of greed being taken to an extreme. They seem to speak to something deep within us, a recognition, perhaps, that given the right circumstances, we too could be tempted to give in to greed.

The Christian Church took a dim view of avarice in medieval and Renaissance times, classifying it as one of the seven deadly sins, and it counselled strongly against falling prey to its lure, recognizing the appeal it could exert on the unwary. Hence the Church's policy on usury, which it denounced as an evil practice that all good Christians should steer well clear of at all times. (Islam continues to oppose usury to this day, generating a very different style of banking in the Islamic world from that in the West, minus interest payments.) When Jews stepped in to provide the service, a love–hate relationship prevailed between borrowers and lenders, as *The Merchant of Venice* makes clear.

The art of the period was attracted to this acknowledged sin as a theme, especially since it had such potential for dramatic portrayal. Hieronymus Bosch's fifteenth-century painting *Death and the Miser*, for example, presents us with a morality tale, in which the dangers of succumbing to greed are made very plain to the viewer. Avarice can lead, the painting warns us, to the loss of our soul, if we are not careful to resist the blandishments of the Devil, who cunningly uses money to lure us to our doom. The scene depicted in the painting is very carefully poised, with an angel pointing out the way to heaven above, showing the sinner that even on his deathbed it is possible for him to repent. But a cunning demon is drawing the man's attention away from the angel by offering him a bag of gold from behind a curtain next to the bed. The man's hand stretches towards the gold, 'almost automatically' by force of a lifetime's habit.[41] In his own mind it is always the case that he lacks enough money; it is for him a 'hole in his being' that he must respond to. At the foot of the bed a figure, thought to represent the miser at an earlier point in his life, is apparently offering a gold coin to a demon, which at the very least is indicative of regular dealings with evil spirits. Meanwhile, death waits expectantly behind the door, and even though the art historian Walter Bosing suggests that 'the issue of the struggle is far from certain', there is a strong implication that the miser will be unable to resist the temptation to accept the gold.[42] His love of riches seems to have corrupted his character to the point where he is probably now incapable of repentance; worldly possessions have cast too much of a spell over him for any sudden transformation to be likely.

This is the story we have found being repeated over and over again throughout this survey, from fictional characters through to real-life entrepreneurs, stock market traders, bankers and corporations: that at some point you just cannot stop; the urge of greed will drive you on. Surrender to avarice and this could be your fate too, is the sombre message being imparted to the Christian audience of Bosch's painting. You may well benefit in this life, but not in the next. You can be sure that your sin will find you out, and when it does, hell is your only possible destination. Bosch was to specialize in scenes of hell, depicting the many horrifying torments that await us if, like his miser, we abandon ourselves on a regular basis to any of the seven deadly sins. Juxtaposed against this, he also presented visions of the heavenly paradise that would be denied to anyone weak enough to give in to sins like avarice, with paradise and hell featuring in several of his panel compositions.

Gluttony was another subject that Bosch kept returning to, as in the *Allegory of Gluttony and Lust* (*c.* 1490–1500), which includes drunkenness as an aspect of the sin. Several characters are pictured flocking eagerly around a wine barrel, and two lovers consume wine together while secreted in a tent away from prying eyes, the viewer being invited to draw the obvious conclusion as to where this unseemliness will lead. Bosing points up the link the artist is expecting us to make: 'that Gluttony and Drunkenness lead to Lust was a lesson that the moralizers never tired of driving home to their audiences.'[43]

Pieter Bruegel the Elder, a sixteenth-century artist influenced by the work of Bosch, produced a series of prints in the late 1550s on the subject of the Seven Deadly Sins, including *Avaritia*, which was made into an engraving by a contemporary of his, Pieter van der Heyden, in 1558 so that its message could be made available to a wider audience. The busy scene depicts various forms of greed, and carries the uncompromising inscription: 'Scraping Avarice sees neither honor nor courtesy, shame nor divine admonition.' It is the same moral that we find in Bosch: you will not escape being punished for this sin in the next world, so take heed of your behaviour and repent while there is still the time and opportunity to do so. Unfortunately if you indulge your sinning nature for long enough, you may find yourself unable to change your ways in time. The various figures in the frame look very much as if they are headed towards this unfortunate fate, and we are expected to condemn their failings, recognizing the peril they are putting their souls in by such displays of 'scraping avarice'. A woman in the foreground sets the tone with a lapful of coins, while next to her a chest full of coins is being filled from a large urn. An animal-faced figure to her left has his arm in a sack full of coins, and elsewhere in the composition scenes of mayhem are depicted – attacks on property, theft and drunken debauchery, for example. The moral import is hard to miss: earthly riches are being privileged over the far more important heavenly kind, which good conduct will open up to the devout believer. Bruegel went on to do a companion series of the seven virtues to point up what such conduct ought to involve.

Divine admonition has not been heeded either by the old woman depicted in Albrecht Dürer's *Avarice* (1507). No doubt once beautiful, but grown withered in appearance with age (the portrait does not spare her in the least, showing her sagging breast, wrinkled face, rough body hair and missing teeth), she clutches a sack of gold coins as if it will somehow protect her from the ravages of time, a rather pathetic '*vanitas* image'.[44] Instead, the action merely demonstrates the depth of her sin and lack of true piety; even at death's door she cannot let go of her greed. As in Bosch's miser, avarice is so engrained in her character that she cannot overcome the habit, despite all the warnings of the Christian clergy as to the inevitability of punishment for this sin in the afterlife. It is a powerful reminder to the viewer of the dangers of over-worldliness: beauty passes, and so does wealth, leaving us with nothing to look forward to at the last but divine judgement. There will be no escape from this for Dürer's woman no matter how much gold she may possess, and overall she cuts both a grotesque and sad figure, someone wilfully blind to her likely spiritual fate.

Anyone who cares to look into works such as these in any detail will find connections being made by art historians to various other paintings of the time, indicating how popular a theme this was for medieval artists. Clearly in medieval society there was a great deal of concern about the Seven Deadly Sins, suggesting that immoral behaviour such as avarice was widespread enough to draw such close attention and open censure. The transience of earthly life as opposed to the eternity of the afterlife was a message that the Christian clergy drummed constantly into their flock, yet apparently even the fear of divine wrath could not eradicate avarice – and if the prospect of an eternity spent in hell was not enough to concentrate the mind, one wonders what would be. It is another demonstration of just how deeply rooted selfishness would appear to be in our psychology, able to override religious belief as well as social disapproval. As we have noted, creative artists have turned to this issue throughout history, right up to the recent filmmakers discussed above. Greed is no less evident in our day than it was in medieval times, and stands just as much in need of censure. Sadly even censure will not deter at least some individuals from following that path and giving in to greed.

CONCLUSION:
LIVING WITH GREED

Greed is a drive that is unlikely to be excised from our culture altogether, certainly not if the free market continues to be the basis of our socioeconomic system (and this is something that shows no indication of changing). The stock market may well be structured around the principles of betting, but the institution is now so well established in our culture that it is hard to envisage life without it. Perhaps we would not want to; it is simply part of the everyday landscape and we have become accustomed to its ways, even if we are apprehensive about where they can sometimes lead. Even those on the left – with a few die-hard exceptions at the militant end of the spectrum (there are still some old-style Marxists around, even after the collapse of the Soviet bloc) – now accept the need for entrepreneurial activity to spur the economy on by increasing GDP. That is always going to involve a certain amount of greed and avarice, because making profit just does. It is difficult to see how wanting to gain more for yourself could not involve greed, even if it is kept at a fairly low level and does not reach the extremes symbolized by the socially unacceptable antics of those classic greedocrats Gordon Gekko and Sherman McCoy. As far as the desire for profit is concerned, demand will keep exceeding need for those committed to the market ethos. How could it do otherwise when the entrepreneurial class is involved? For them it is the natural way to behave, and they seem unable to conceive of the world differently. Everything is to be judged on a financial basis; every human activity is to be seen in terms of profit and loss.

Profit and greed are phenomena we must therefore learn to cope with, although they can be subjected to controls in the name of the public good – despite the continued protestations of the neoliberal lobby. They will have to be subjected to such controls if we want to move towards a more stable and egalitarian society, without the rapidly growing discrepancy between rich and poor that we are currently witnessing. The longer this trend goes on, the more our society will be put at risk by rising social tensions. The anti-capitalist movement is only the tip of the iceberg in this respect: public disapproval goes much deeper than the champions of neoliberalism are willing to acknowledge. As Thomas Piketty has pointed out, fiscal consent (that is, agreeing to abide by your country's tax laws) cannot go on being undermined indefinitely, not without causing serious damage to the liberal democratic political system that has come to be the norm in the West, and that still has the support of the vast majority of its citizens. The market is an integral part of that settlement, but that does not mean it has to be the final arbiter of all human activity within our culture, or that market values must be the standard by which all others are to be measured; we can choose a different way of going about things. I am arguing that we have reached the stage when we must, when our social health critically depends upon it.

The last financial crisis could have been avoided if an appropriate system of monitoring had been in place, rather than being systematically dismantled in line with the current economic dogma of neoliberalism and its anti-regulation bias. The more regulations of the financial industry have been loosened, the greater have been the swings on the market and throughout the global economy, to the detriment of quality of life for the general population. This is a connection that seems horribly obvious to everyone except those in the industry itself, who are determined to carry on as if nothing has happened. No one is seriously recommending a loosening of controls when it comes to international sports such as athletics and cycling, well aware of how the greed for fame can drastically distort individuals' moral sense, as it did with multiple Tour de France winner Lance Armstrong and several Olympic medallists (a list that is growing as investigations press on). The doping scandals and corruption charges with which we are now being daily regaled ought to provide a lasting lesson in just how far we can trust individual ambition when there is a lot at stake. Yet when it comes to greed for financial gain by traders and bankers unconcerned at its effect on others, we are being asked to believe that everyone involved in the financial industry will act responsibly and exercise their social conscience, without any outside auditing, despite a mountain of evidence to the contrary. Nice as it would undoubtedly be to feel able to believe in the essential goodness of humankind, it has to be acknowledged that antisocial traits will keep breaking through unless we are extremely vigilant. Without some tight controls, greed will mushroom, as it has been doing for some time now. Hobbes was right, up to a point: selfishness has to be kept in check.

Given the addictive attraction posed by the stock market, the greedy will continue to join its ranks; this appears to be a sad fact of existence. Yet that need not mean they cannot be held in check, as we know they have to be when it comes to the sports just mentioned. That, too, appears to be a fact of existence. There very definitely should be limits set as to how far the members of the trading fraternity are allowed to go in the pursuit of stock market gains. 'Masters of the Universe' need to be taken down a peg or two for the protection of the general public. Laissez-faire does not have to be interpreted quite so literally as has become the convention in the financial industry. That particular interpretation relies far more than is safe on goodwill, which is not as widespread a trait among humanity as some of us would like to believe. Perhaps the best we can hope for is that greed can be reduced from its present levels, but this is still a goal worth pursuing. We must attempt to achieve the right degree of tension between competing drives, such as demand and need, and this must remain an ongoing process in this, as in any, society.

We have to accept that for the truly driven entrepreneur – and there are quite a few of them around – no financial gain is ever going to be enough; thus the popularity among this group of tax avoidance schemes, despite their antisocial implications. Some successful entrepreneurs may engage in large-scale philanthropic schemes, as Bill Gates has done; Linsey McGoey has denounced such efforts as 'philanthrocapitalism', claiming they are often little better than vanity projects. And it is a further objection that much of the funding for projects of this nature could well have been generated by tax avoidance anyway. The depressing truth is that what successful entrepreneurs feel they lack, is more. Characters of this nature will rarely be satisfied, or at least not for very long. In this world, excess must lead to yet more excess, *ad infinitum*; though those pursuing it so single-mindedly hardly recognize it as excess. The character of Curtis Jadwin in Norris's novel *The Pit* provides a classic fictional portrait of the process in action. He illustrates how greed can override any cut-off mechanism an individual may have, driving them on either to greater success or, as Jadwin discovers, to comprehensive financial disaster. This is the 'boom and bust' cycle busily at work within the individual, and it would seem to be encoded in the market mentality to go for broke at all times – the demand greed will make of all those who are tempted to follow its call. In the entrepreneurial world trading figures must be improved year on year, profits must accrue faster and faster than before, the enterprise must never let up. If it does then shareholders will look around for more lucrative stocks in which to invest, as the search for higher returns never ceases. It then becomes a question of how to safeguard wider society from the excesses that greed can lead to if it is given free rein, and that is where government has to step in and take decisive action. Where excess is seen as a virtue, we cannot continue to have faith that the 'invisible hand' will come to the rescue. It manifestly failed to do so in the Wall Street crash of 1929 or the credit crisis of 2007–8.

The question arises as to whom governments should favour in their overall economic policy: shareholders or stakeholders? After the experiences of the last financial crash it appears that an uncontrolled financial sector is simply asking for trouble. Only elected governments, under persistent prompting from the wider electorate (who will ultimately have to suffer the most in such situations), have the power to impose and monitor restrictions on the sector for the general social good – including the good of the nation's economy. Self-regulation has not been found effective. We know from the existence, and persistence, of crime, that it is naive to assume this innate goodness; that is why we have police forces to ensure at least some security. Appropriate legislation and regular, rigorous auditing on the part of the authorities are therefore the first requirements in finding a way to accommodate greed. Education can play its part too in encouraging and making clear the virtues of social responsibility in all our actions, and if it seems very basic to be making such a point, it is because experience suggests that all too frequently the financial sector is only paying lip service to this idea. What those involved say, and what they do, differ, and often quite starkly. Now that entrepreneurship is making its way onto school and university syllabi as a topic, let us hope that social responsibility is always seen to be an essential part of the teaching and learning package.

The same apparently applies throughout much of the world of international sport, where in far too many cases social respons-ibility seems to be a disturbingly low priority for participants, as evidenced by the widespread use of performance-enhancing drugs by Russian Olympic athletes. Russia has since made counter-claims about many Western athletes, so the story goes on. Nor is it ever enough to claim that this is just the custom of sporting institutions, that this is the way that 'selfish passions' work and we must go along with it. Adam Smith, for one, would never have accepted that, asserting forcefully that when custom is used to justify such behaviour,

> we may well imagine that there is scarce any particular practice so gross which it cannot authorise. Such a thing, we hear men every day saying, is commonly done, and they seem to think this a sufficient apology for what, in itself, is the most unjust and unreasonable conduct.[1]

Custom is a poor excuse, especially when it is used to justify corrupt practices. Monopolies, too, are the product of custom within large organizations, but that does not make the practice right. Customs can be changed; they are not set in stone for eternity, otherwise societies would remain stuck at a low level of development indefinitely.

Perhaps greed, like the poor, is destined always to be with us. Our psychology would, unfortunately, imply that this is so. However, that does not mean that we have to consider ourselves as being captive to greed (as Mother Courage appears to feel she is) any more than we should stop trying to alleviate poverty and bring about a more equal society. Or, for that matter, calling for reform of the system that allows tax avoidance to thrive in the face of public disapproval. Tax havens merely encourage greed, and they will have to be dealt with sooner or later by the major Western nations. 'Theft pure and simple' should not be receiving the kind of official protection it now is, no matter how tacit that may be; nor should it even be possible to engage in the practice of 'profit shifting'. Governments must be held to account for any promises they make to reform the system, otherwise the 'hidden wealth of nations' will continue to be hidden from where it should really be circulating: in the public realm, funding projects and systems that make life better for everyone. For there to be such reserves of 'hidden wealth' in an era of austerity is completely unacceptable, just one more 'custom' that has been allowed to develop despite its manifest unfairness. To let this continue is to show contempt for the stakeholder population at large, and that is a group that is hard-pressed enough as it is. Greed's wilder excesses, and the effect they are having on the body politic, must be flagged up as frequently as possible. Our journey through the history of greed confirms that it is clearly not in society's interest for the trait to go unchecked.

Neither is greed imposed on us from without; it comes from within us, which means that we need to maintain a constant watch for the phenomenon, because the capacity for it is part of our make-up and we will continue to encounter it in the course of our everyday business with others. Institutions do not create greed, or the 'secret religion for the super-rich' either. We cannot blame the stock market, neoliberal economics or FIFA for the actions of individuals, as organizations could be made subject to far stricter codes of conduct by appropriate legislation. Organizations merely provide the opportunity for individuals to express and satisfy their greed, which can soon become entrenched there, rather like a disease creeping through the system and infecting everyone who comes into contact with it. Before long, it is being defended as custom and taken for granted as just the way of the world. A culture of greed is above all a human creation, and it has to be addressed at that level.

It is impossible not to note an ideological dimension when discussing greed, in that those in positions of authority (whether financial, managerial or political) do provide the most obvious examples of greed in action, as we have consistently seen through-out this survey. Directing our anger at these particular individuals, understandable though that would be, is to miss the main point. They are simply exercising a trait present within all of us, in a system that is open to being manipulated because of a lack of robust mon-itoring, and our present-day culture strongly encourages personal accumulation. If we put the the trait and the system together, we soon find ourselves confronted by some quite breathtaking cases of greed perpetrated by self-styled 'Masters of the Universe', seemingly devoid of social conscience. In the highly competitive, market-based culture we have developed in the modern era, human nature will almost inevitably gravitate towards this state of affairs; that is, unless we take some positive action to curb the opportunities for excess that we know will always arise in any context where there is a large amount of money involved. We must take positive action, too, against the drives that propel individuals towards seeking that excess, because we know that left to their own devices they will recognize no limits and keep testing just how far they can go, how many demands they are allowed to make without being reined in. Unfortunately desire cannot be relied upon to regulate itself.

We come back to the issue of deferred gratification, and the trend towards regarding this as the enemy of desire. Sometimes it is necessary to sound a moralistic note about such things. The commercial world is very obviously out to banish deferred gratification from our lives, and while it does not as such create greed, it definitely gives it a framework in which to flourish – and it has been flourishing. Greed means we want things now, instantly, to fill what we have convinced ourselves is a 'hole in our being'; whether it be to make a killing on the stock market, or more and more of whatever it is that we happen to be addicted to – food, clothes, technology or luxuries. That addiction, however, is rarely only a private matter; it has multiple social consequences, and it calls for a concerted response to prevent it from getting seriously out of hand. We may well have to live with greed, but the task that lies before us is to ensure that it is kept within reasonable bounds – and, even more importantly, to decide just what those bounds are, where the demands of the greedocracy must stop. It is a delicate balance to achieve, but the social benefits it will bring can hardly be over-estimated. 'Masters of the Universe', of whatever form or persuasion, may demur, but there just has to be more to existence than unrestricted accumulation.

REFERENCES

Introduction: Why is Greed an Issue?

1 Frank Norris, *McTeague: A Story of San Francisco* [1899] (New York, 2011), p. 34.
2 Tom Wolfe, *The Bonfire of the Vanities* (London, 1988), p. 19.
3 Paul Mason, *Meltdown: The End of the Age of Greed* (London and New York, 2009), p. 128.
4 Ibid.
5 Paul Krugman, *The Return of Depression Economics and the Crisis of 2008* (London, 2008), p. 180.
6 Charles Dickens, *A Christmas Carol and The Chimes* [1843, 1844] (London, 1977), p. 10.
7 Michael Pye, *The Edge of the World: How the North Sea Made Us Who We Are* (London, 2015), p. 218.
8 David Smith, Ben Jacobs and Sabrina Siddiqui, 'Crisis for Republican Party as Trump Heads for Super Tuesday Victory', www.theguardian.com, 1 March 2016.

1 To Defend or Not to Defend Greed?

1 Stewart Sutherland, *Greed: From Gordon Gekko to David Hume* (London, 2014), p. 6.
2 Tore Renberg, *See You Tomorrow*, trans. Seán Kinsella (London, 2014), p. 110.
3 Bertolt Brecht, *The Threepenny Opera* [1928], trans. Desmond I. Vesey and Eric Bentley (New York, 1994), p. 5.
4 John Gay, *The Beggar's Opera* [1728], ed. Edgar V. Roberts (London, 1969), p. 6.
5 Ibid., pp. 6–7.

6 Bertolt Brecht and Kurt Weill, *The Rise and Fall of the City of Mahagonny* [1930], trans. Michael Feingold (libretto accompanying 1988 Capriccio CD recording).
7 Bertolt Brecht, *The Threepenny Novel* [1934], trans. Desmond I. Vesey and Christopher Isherwood (Harmondsworth, 1961), p. 30.

2 Whatever You Desire? The Psychology of Greed

1 C. B. Macpherson, *The Political Theory of Possessive Individualism: Hobbes to Locke* (Oxford, 1962), p. 3.
2 See Michel Foucault, *The History of Sexuality*, vols I–III [1976, 1984, 1984], trans. Robert Hurley (Harmondsworth, 1981, 1987, 1990).
3 Gilles Deleuze and Félix Guattari, *Anti-Oedipus: Capitalism and Schizophrenia* [1972], trans. Robert Hurley et al. (London, 1983), p. 2.
4 Sigmund Freud, 'Further Remarks on the Neuro-Psychoses of Defence' [1896], in *Standard Edition of the Complete Psychological Works of Sigmund Freud*, trans. and ed. James Strachey (London, 1953–74), vol. III, p. 170.
5 Sigmund Freud and Josef Breuer, 'Studies in Hysteria' [1893–5], in *Standard Edition*, vol. II, pp. 122–3.
6 Thomas De Quincey, *Confessions of an English Opium Eater* [1821–2], ed. Barry Milligan (London, 2003).
7 Thomas Hobbes, *Leviathan, or, The Matter, Forme and Power of a Free Common-wealth* [1651], ed. C. B. Macpherson (Harmondsworth, 1968), p. 186.
8 Deleuze and Guattari, *Anti-Oedipus*, p. 5.
9 Paul Verhaeghe, *On Being Normal and Other Disorders: A Manual for Clinical Psychodiagnostics*, trans. Sigi Jottkandt (London, 2008), p. 8.
10 Deleuze and Guattari, *Anti-Oedipus*, p. 3.
11 Mark Seem, 'Introduction', in Deleuze and Guattari, *Anti-Oedipus*, p. xvii.
12 Deleuze and Guattari, *Anti-Oedipus*, pp. 8, 10.
13 See Stuart Sim, *Fifty Key Postmodern Thinkers* (London and New York, 2013), p. 73.
14 See Gilles Deleuze and Félix Guattari, *A Thousand Plateaus: Capitalism and Schizophrenia* [1980], trans. Brian Massumi (London, 1988).

15 Verhaeghe, *On Being Normal*, p. 8.

16 Robert Bocock, *Sigmund Freud* (London and New York, 1983), p. 42.

17 Freud and Breuer, 'Studies in Hysteria', p. xxix.

18 Ibid., p. 246.

19 Freud, 'The Question of Lay Analysis' [1926], in *Standard Edition*, vol. xx, p. 212.

20 See Juliet Mitchell, *Psychoanalysis and Feminism: A Radical Reassessment of Freudian Psychoanalysis* (London, 1974), p. xv.

21 Madan Sarup, *Jacques Lacan* (Toronto and Buffalo, 1992), p. 13.

22 Jacques Lacan, *The Four Fundamental Concepts of Psycho-analysis* [1973], ed. Jacques-Alain Miller, trans. Alan Sheridan (London, 1994), pp. 38, 204.

23 Bruce Fink, Preface to Jacques Lacan, *The Seminar of Jacques Lacan, Book xx: On Feminine Sexuality, the Limits of Love and Knowledge* [1975], ed. Jacques-Alain Miller, trans. Bruce Fink (New York, 1999), p. vii.

24 Lacan ibid., p. 73.

25 Jacques Lacan, *Ecrits: A Selection*, trans. Alan Sheridan (London and New York, 1989), p. 263.

3 In the Red Corner, Karl Marx; in the Blue, Adam Smith: The Economics of Greed

1 Adam Smith, *An Inquiry into the Nature and Causes of the Wealth of Nations, Books I–III* [1776], ed. R. H. Campbell et al. (Oxford, 1976), p. 251.

2 Ibid., p. 164.

3 Ibid., p. 456.

4 Joseph E. Stiglitz, *Globalization and Its Discontents* (London, 2002), p. 74.

5 Ibid.

6 Adam Smith, *The Theory of Moral Sentiments* [1759], ed. D. D. Raphael and A. L. MacFie (Oxford, 1976), p. 9.

7 D. D. Raphael and A. L. McFie, 'Introduction', in Smith, *Theory of Moral Sentiments*, pp. 1–52 (p. 6).

8 Smith, *Theory of Moral Sentiments*, p. 25.

9 Ibid., pp. 140–41.

10 Smith, *Wealth of Nations*, p. 430.

11 Ibid.

12 Pierre-Joseph Proudhon, *What is Property? An Inquiry into the*

Principle and Right of Government [1840], trans. Benjamin R. Tucker (London, n.d.), vol. I, p. 38.

13 Karl Marx and Friedrich Engels, *The Communist Manifesto* [1848], ed. Frederic L. Bender (New York and London, 1988), p. 75.

14 Karl Marx and Friedrich Engels, *The German Ideology* [1845] (London, 1965), p. 45.

15 Richard Murphy, *The Joy of Tax: How a Fair Tax System Can Create a Better Society* (London, 2015), p. 16.

16 Thomas Piketty, Foreword to Gabriel Zucman, *The Hidden Wealth of Nations: The Scourge of Tax Havens*, trans. Teresa Lavender Fagan (Chicago, IL, and London, 2015), p. viii.

17 Zucman, *The Hidden Wealth of Nations*, p. 4.

18 Ibid., p. 1.

19 Ibid., pp. 92, 93.

20 Ibid., p. 79.

21 Linsey McGoey, *No Such Thing as a Free Gift: The Gates Foundation and the Price of Philanthropy* (London and New York, 2015).

22 Protestants in England in the seventeenth and eighteenth centuries who refused to conform to the state's established church, the Anglican, were barred from careers in the universities or the law. Many of these 'nonconformists' turned to the world of trade instead, and were prone to regard success there as evidence of God's approval and support for their cause.

4 A World Fit for Shareholders: Greed and the Financial Industry

1 See Milton Friedman, *Capitalism and Freedom*, 2nd edn (Chicago, IL, and London, 1982).

2 See Richard Wachman, 'Dutch Bankers' Bonuses Axed by People Power', *The Observer* (27 March 2011), p. 46.

3 Thomas Piketty, *Capital in the Twenty-first Century*, trans. Arthur Goldhammer (Cambridge, MA, 2014), p. 23.

4 Ibid., p. 1.

5 Ibid., p. 530.

6 Quoted in Jana Kasparkevic, 'When Wealth is Bad for Your Health: The 1% Turn to Therapy', *The Observer* (17 October 2015), p. 43.

7 Ibid.

8 See Guy Standing, *The Precariat: The New Dangerous Class* (London, 2011).

5 Food, Greed and Consequences

1 Walter Bosing, *Hieronymus Bosch, c. 1450–1516: Between Heaven and Hell* (Cologne, 1987), p. 30.

2 The mockery is carried to a hilarious extreme in the Monty Python film *The Meaning of Life* (1983), where a glutton is plied with food in a restaurant to the point where he explodes.

3 BMI (body mass index) is calculated on the basis of weight in kilograms over height squared (in centimetres).

4 Branwen Jeffreys, 'Maternal Deaths Linked to Obesity', www.news.bbc.co.uk, 4 December 2007.

5 Nicola Heslehurst et al., 'An Evaluation of the Implementation of Maternal Obesity Pathways of Care: A Mixed Methods Study with Data Integration', *PLOS One* (May 2015), pp. 1–21 (p. 21).

6 Ibid.

7 Jeffreys, 'Maternal Deaths Linked to Obesity'.

8 See Bee Wilson, *First Bite: How We Learn to Eat* (London, 2015).

9 Marta Zaraska, 'Bitter Truth: Fruit and Veg are Getting Tastier . . . at the Expense of Our Health', *New Scientist*, 3032 (1 August 2015), pp. 26–30.

10 Jennifer McLagan, *Bitter: A Taste of the World's Most Dangerous Flavor, With Recipes* (Berkeley, CA, 2014), p. 137.

11 See, for example, the fact sheet put out by the American National Cancer Institute ('Cruciferous Vegetables and Cancer Prevention', www.cancer.gov, accessed 11 November 2015), which briefly glosses the findings of several studies on the topic.

12 David Kessler, *The End of Overeating: Taking Control of the Insatiable American Appetite* (New York, 2009).

13 Quoted in Joanna Moorhead, 'Diabetes: The Scourge of City Living', *The Guardian* (13 January 2016), p. 40.

14 Felicity Lawrence, *Eat Your Heart Out: Why the Food Business is Bad for the Planet and Your Health* (London, 2009), p. x.

15 Mike C. Parent and Jessica L. Alquist, 'Born Fat: The Relations Between Weight Changeability Beliefs and Health Behaviors and Physical Health', *Health Education and Behavior*, XLIII/3 (8 September 2015), pp. 337–46.

6 A Bitter Pill? Healthcare and Greed

1 'Keep Our NHS Public', www.keepournhspublic.com, accessed
   19 November 2015.
2 See Susan Carroll, 'Senior Day-trippers Seeking Fun, Cheap
   Prescriptions', *Banderas News*, www.banderasnews.com, April 2005.
3 Harmony Huskinson, 'Americans Find Huge Savings from
   Pharmacies, Dentists Based in Canada and Mexico', *Two Borders*
   (Cronkite Borderlands Initiative), https://cronkite.asu.edu,
   24 September 2013.
4 See 'IVF', *NHS Choices*, www.nhs.uk (accessed 30 September 2015).
5 Harriet Meyer, 'Egg Freezing is the Tempting Option if You're
   Desperate for a Child: But Can Women Be Sure it's the Right
   Choice?', *The Observer* (25 October 2015), pp. 8–9.
6 See 'Genetic Test is Back', *New Scientist*, 3045 (31 October 2015),
   p. 7.
7 'Feedback', *New Scientist*, 3050 (5 December 2015), p. 56.
8 Ibid.
9 Ibid.
10 Richard Feynman, *The Character of Physical Law* [1965] (London,
   1992), p. 129.
11 'Feedback', *New Scientist*, 3055 (9 January 2016), p. 56.

7 From Colonialism to Neocolonialism: The Politics and Geopolitics of Greed

1 Tim Marshall, *Prisoners of Geography: Ten Maps that Tell You
   Everything You Need to Know About Global Politics* (London, 2015),
   p. 50.
2 Ibid., p. 103.
3 World War 1 Document Archive, '1911: David Lloyd George
   Delivers Mansion House Speech', http://.wwi.lib.byu.edu,
   accessed 29 October 2015.
4 Thomas Piketty, *Capital in the Twenty-first Century*, trans. Arthur
   Goldhammer (Cambridge, MA, 2014), p. 539.
5 Joseph Conrad, *Heart of Darkness* [1902] (Harmondsworth, 1973),
   p. 10.
6 Ibid.
7 Adam Hochschild, *King Leopold's Ghost: A Story of Greed, Terror
   and Heroism* (New York, 1998), p. 3.

8 Marshall, *Prisoners of Geography*, p. 105.
9 Edward Said, *Orientalism* (Harmondsworth, 1985), p. 7.
10 E. M. Forster, *A Passage to India* [1924], ed. Oliver Stallybrass (Harmondsworth, 1979), pp. 79–80.
11 Conrad, *Heart of Darkness*, p. 23.
12 Roland Barthes, *Mythologies* [1957], trans. Annette Lavers (London, 1973), p. 68.
13 Niall Ferguson, *Empire: How Britain Made the Modern World* (London, 2002), p. xxvi.
14 Ibid., p. 74.
15 V. I. Lenin, *Imperialism: The Highest Stage of Capitalism* (Peking, 1975), p. 4.
16 D. K. Fieldhouse, *Economics and Empire, 1830–1914* (London, 1984), p. 7.
17 Ferguson, *Empire*, p. 51.
18 Ibid., p. 217.
19 Fieldhouse, *Economics and Empire*, p. 87.
20 Ibid., p. 223.

8 International Sport and the Greed for Fame and Success

1 The reporter Andrew Jennings has specialized in investigating FIFA's tangled financial affairs. His latest book on the subject is *The Dirty Game: Uncovering the Scandal at FIFA* (London, 2015).
2 Dave Zinn, 'Throw FIFA Out of the Game', *New York Times*, 6 June 2014, www.nytimes.com.
3 In an American sporting context, baseball would offer comparable opportunities.
4 Sean Ingle, 'Revealed: Tennis Umpires Secretly Banned over Tennis Scam', *The Guardian*, 9 February 2016.
5 The whole rather sordid story of Armstrong's downfall is recounted in David Walsh, *From Lance to Landis: Inside the American Doping Controversy at the Tour de France* (New York, 2007).

9 The Art of Greed

1 James Shapiro, *Shakespeare and the Jews* (New York and Chichester, 1996), p. 130.
2 Ibid.

3 William Shakespeare, *The Merchant of Venice* [1596–8], ed. John Drakakis (London, 2010), 4.i, pp. 358–9.

4 Alan Sinfield, *Faultlines: Cultural Materialism and the Politics of Dissident Reading* (Oxford, 1992), pp. 301.

5 Ibid.

6 Ibid., p. 302.

7 Ibid., p. 301.

8 Ben Jonson, *Volpone, or The Foxe* [1605], in *Five Plays*, ed. G. A. Wilkes (Oxford, 1988), I.i, l. 1–2, p. 231.

9 Ibid., I.i, l. 73–81, p. 233.

10 Ibid., I.i, l. 86, p. 233.

11 Ibid., I.ii, l. 87–91, p. 237.

12 Molière, *The Miser* [1668], in *The Miser and Other Plays*, trans. John Wood (London, 1962), p. 171.

13 Ibid., p. 123.

14 Ibid., p. 112.

15 Ibid., p. 131.

16 Bertolt Brecht, *Mother Courage and Her Children: A Chronicle of the Thirty Years War* [1941], trans. Eric Bentley (London, 1962), p. 26.

17 Ibid., p. 81.

18 Charles Dickens, *A Christmas Carol and The Chimes* [1843, 1844], (London, 1977), p. 10.

19 Ibid., p. 81.

20 Ibid., pp. 14, 15.

21 Charles Dickens, *Hard Times: For These Times* [1854], ed. David Craig (Harmondsworth, 1969), p. 67.

22 Ibid., p. 65.

23 Thomas Carlyle, 'Chartism' [1839], in *Selected Essays*, ed. Ian Campbell (London, 1972), pp. 165–238 (p. 205).

24 Frank Norris, *McTeague: A Story of San Francisco* [1899] (New York, 2011), p. 165.

25 Ibid., p. 36.

26 Ibid., p. 34.

27 Ibid.

28 Ibid., p. 11.

29 Eric Solomon, 'Introduction' to *McTeague* (New York, 2011), pp. vii–xviii (p. xviii).

30 Frank Norris, *The Octopus: A Story of California* [1901] (Marston Gate, 2015), p. 306.

31 Ibid., p. 15.
32 Ibid., p. 577.
33 Ibid., p. 48.
34 Frank Norris, *The Pit: A Story of Chicago* [1903] (Marston Gate, 2015), pp. xxviii–xxix.
35 Ibid., p. l.
36 Ibid., p. lix.
37 George Packer, *The Unwinding: An Inner History of the New America* (London, 2013), p. 3.
38 See Jordan Belfort, *The Wolf of Wall Street* (New York, 2007).
39 Seth Freedman, *Binge Trading: The Real Inside Story of Cash, Cocaine and Corruption in the City* (London, 2009), pp. 24–5.
40 Michael Lewis, *The Big Short: Inside the Doomsday Machine* (London, 2011), p. 242.
41 Walter Bosing, *Hieronymus Bosch, c. 1450–1516: Between Heaven and Hell* (Cologne, 1987), p. 32.
42 Ibid.
43 Ibid.
44 Martin Bailey, *Dürer* (London, 1995), p. 13.

Conclusion: Living with Greed

1 Adam Smith, *The Theory of Moral Sentiments* [1759], ed. D. D. Raphael and A. L. MacFie (Oxford, 1976), p. 210.

BIBLIOGRAPHY

Bailey, Martin, *Dürer* (London, 1995)

Barthes, Roland, *Mythologies* [1957], trans. Annette Lavers (London, 1973)

Bocock, Robert, *Sigmund Freud* (London and New York, 1983)

Bosing, Walter, *Hieronymus Bosch, c. 1450–1516: Between Heaven and Hell* (Cologne, 1987)

Brecht, Bertolt, *The Threepenny Opera* [1928], trans. Desmond I. Vesey and Eric Bentley (New York, 1994)

—, *The Threepenny Novel* [1934], trans. Desmond I. Vesey and Christopher Isherwood (Harmondsworth, 1961)

—, *Mother Courage and Her Children: A Chronicle of the Thirty Years War* [1941], trans. Eric Bentley (London, 1962)

Carlyle, Thomas, 'Chartism' [1829], in *Selected Essays*, ed. Ian Campbell (London, 1972), pp. 165–238

Carroll, Susan, 'Senior Day-trippers Seeking Fun, Cheap Prescriptions', *Banderas News*, www.banderasnews.com, April 2005

Conrad, Joseph, *Heart of Darkness* [1902] (Harmondsworth, 1973)

Deleuze, Gilles, and Félix Guattari, *Anti-Oedipus: Capitalism and Schizophrenia* [1972], trans. Robert Hurley et al. (London, 1983)

Dickens, Charles, *A Christmas Carol and The Chimes* [1843, 1844] (London, 1977)

—, *Hard Times: For These Times* [1854], ed. David Craig (Harmondsworth, 1969)

'Feedback', *New Scientist*, 3050 (5 December 2015), p. 56

Ferguson, Niall, *Empire: How Britain Made the Modern World* (London, 2002)

Feynman, Richard, *The Character of Physical Law* [1965] (London, 1992)

Fieldhouse, D. K., *Economics and Empire, 1830–1914* (London and Basingstoke, 1984)

Forster, E. M., *A Passage to India* [1924], ed. Oliver Stallybrass (Harmondsworth, 1979)

Freedman, Seth, *Binge Trading: The Real Inside Story of Cash, Cocaine and Corruption in the City* (London, 2009)

Freud, Sigmund, *Standard Edition of the Complete Psychological Works of Sigmund Freud*, vols I–XXIV, trans. and ed. James Strachey (London, 1953–74)

Gay, John, *The Beggar's Opera* [1728], ed. Edgar V. Roberts (London, 1969)

'Genetic Test is Back', *New Scientist*, 3045 (31 October 2015), p. 7

Heslehurst, Nicola, et al., 'An Evaluation of the Implementation of Maternal Obesity Pathways of Care: A Mixed Methods Study with Data Integration', *PLoS One* (27 May 2015), pp. 1–21

Hobbes, Thomas, *Leviathan, or, The Matter, Forme, and Power of a Free Common-wealth Ecclesiasticall and Civill* [1651], ed. C. B. Macpherson (Harmondsworth, 1968)

Hochschild, Adam, *King Leopold's Ghost: A Story of Greed, Terror and Heroism in Colonial Africa* (New York, 1998)

Huskinson, Harmony, 'Americans Find Huge Savings from Pharmacies, Dentists Based in Canada and Mexico', *Two Borders* (Cronkite Borderlands Initiative), https://cronkite.asu.edu, 24 September 2013

Jeffreys, Branwen, 'Maternal Deaths Linked to Obesity', www.bbc.co.uk/news, 4 December 2007

Jonson, Ben, *Volpone, or The Foxe* [1605], in *Five Plays*, ed. G. A. Wilkes (Oxford, 1988)

Kasperkevic, Jana, 'When Wealth is Bad for Your Health: The 1% Turn to Therapy', *The Observer* (17 October 2015), p. 43

'Keep Our NHS Public', www.keepournhspublic.com, accessed 19 November 2015

Krugman, Paul, *The Return of Depression Economics and the Crisis of 2008* (London, 2008)

Lacan, Jacques, *Écrits: A Selection*, trans. Alan Sheridan (London and New York, 1989)

—, *Four Fundamental Concepts of Psychoanalysis* [1973], ed. Jacques-Alain Miller, trans. Alan Sheridan (London, 1994)

—, *The Seminar of Jacques Lacan, Book XX: On Feminine Sexuality, The Limits of Love and Knowledge* [1975], ed. Jacques-Alain Miller, trans. Bruce Fink (New York, 1999)

Lawrence, Felicity, *Eat Your Heart Out: Why the Food Business is Bad for the Planet and Your Health* (London, 2009)

Lenin, V. I., *Imperialism, the Highest Stage of Capitalism* [1917] (Peking, 1975)

Lewis, Michael, *The Big Short: Inside the Doomsday Machine* (London, 2011)

McLagan, Jennifer, *Bitter: A Taste of the World's Most Dangerous Flavor, With Recipes* (Berkeley, CA, 2014)

Macpherson, C. B., *The Political Theory of Possessive Individualism: Hobbes to Locke* (Oxford, 1962)

Marshall, Tim, *Prisoners of Geography: Ten Maps that Tell You Everything You Need to Know about Global Politics* (London, 2015)

Marx, Karl, *Capital: A Critique of Political Economy*, vol. 1 [1867], trans. Ben Fowkes (Harmondsworth, 1976)

—, and Friedrich Engels, *The German Ideology* [1845] (London, 1965)

—, and Friedrich Engels, *The Communist Manifesto* [1848], ed. Frederic L. Bender (New York and London, 1988)

Mason, Paul, *Meltdown: The End of the Age of Greed* (London and New York, 2009)

Meyer, Harriet, 'Egg Freezing is the Tempting Option if You're Desperate for a Child: But Can Women Be Sure it's the Right Choice?', *The Observer* (25 October 2015), pp. 8–9

Mitchell, Juliet, *Psychoanalysis and Feminism: A Radical Reassessment of Freudian Psychoanalysis* (London, 1974)

Molière, *The Miser* [1668], in *The Miser and Other Plays*, trans. John Wood (London, 1962)

Moorhead, Joanna, 'Diabetes: The Scourge of City Living', *The Guardian* (13 January 2016), p. 40

Murphy, Richard, *The Joy of Tax: How a Fair Tax System Can Create a Better Society* (London, 2015)

National Cancer Institute, 'Cruciferous Vegetables and Cancer Prevention', www.cancer.gov, accessed 11 November 2015

Norris, Frank, *McTeague: A Story of San Francisco* [1899] (New York, 2011)

—, *The Octopus: A Story of California* [1901] (Marston Gate, 2015)

—, *The Pit: A Story of Chicago* [1903] (Marston Gate, 2015)

Packer, George, *The Unwinding: An Inner History of the New America* (London, 2013)

Parent, Mike C., and Jessica L. Alquist, 'Born Fat: The Relations Between Weight Changeability Beliefs and Health Behaviors and Physical Health', *Health Education and Behavior*, XLIII/3 (8 September 2015), pp. 337–46

Piketty, Thomas, *Capital in the Twenty-first Century*, trans. Arthur Goldhammer (Cambridge, MA, 2014)

Proudhon, Pierre-Joseph, *What is Property? An Inquiry into the Principle and Right of Government* [1840], trans. Benjamin R. Tucker (London, n.d.)

Pye, Michael, *The Edge of the World: How the North Sea Made Us Who We Are* (London, 2015)

Renberg, Tore, *See You Tomorrow*, trans. Seán Kinsella (London, 2014)

Said, Edward, *Orientalism* (Harmondsworth, 1985)

Sarup, Madan, *Jacques Lacan* (Toronto and Buffalo, NY, 1992)

Shakespeare, William, *The Merchant of Venice* [1596–8], ed. John Drakakis (London, 2010)

Shapiro, James, *Shakespeare and the Jews* (New York and Chichester, 1996)

Sim, Stuart, *Fifty Key Postmodern Thinkers* (London and New York, 2013)

Sinfield, Alan, *Faultlines: Cultural Materialism and the Politics of Dissident Reading* (Oxford, 1992)

Smith, Adam, *The Theory of Moral Sentiments* [1759], ed. D. D. Raphael and A. L. MacFie (Oxford, 1976)

—, *An Inquiry into the Nature and Causes of the Wealth of Nations, Books I–III* [1776], ed. R. H. Campbell et al. (Oxford, 1976)

Smith, David, Ben Jacobs and Sabrina Siddiqui, 'Crisis for Republican Party as Trump Heads for Super Tuesday Victory', *The Guardian*, www.theguardian.com, 1 March 2016

Stiglitz, Joseph E., *Globalization and its Discontents* (London, 2002)

Sutherland, Stuart, *Greed: From Gordon Gekko to David Hume* (London, 2014)

Verhaeghe, Paul, *On Being Normal and Other Disorders: A Manual for Clinical Psychodiagnostics*, trans. Sigi Jottkandt (London, 2008)

Wolfe, Tom, *The Bonfire of the Vanities* (London, 1988)

World War I Document Archive, '1911: David Lloyd George Delivers Mansion House Speech', https://wwi.lib.byu.edu, accessed 29 October 2015

Zaraska, Marta, 'Bitter Truth: Fruit and Veg are Getting Tastier . . . at the Expense of Our Health', *New Scientist*, 3032 (2015), pp. 26–30

Zucman, Gabriel, *The Hidden Wealth of Nations: The Scourge of Tax Havens*, trans. Teresa Lavender Fagan (Chicago, IL, and London, 2015)

ACKNOWLEDGEMENTS

Ben Hayes at Reaktion suggested the topic, and was very helpful in getting the project off the ground and into its final form. Dr Helene Brandon provided invaluable help on the medical matters discussed in the book and, as always, was the sounding board for its various arguments over the course of its writing.

INDEX